The
ⓐ*rchers*
ⓐ*narchists'*

SURVIVAL GUIDE

The
ⓐrchers
ⓐnarchists'

SURVIVAL
GUIDE

IAN SANDERSON

First published 1999 by **Boxtree**
an imprint of **Macmillan Publishers Ltd**
25 Eccleston Place London SW1W 9NF
Basingstoke and Oxford

www.macmillan.co.uk

Associated companies throughout the world

ISBN 0 7522 1805 0

Text © **Ian Sanderson** 1999

9 8 7 6 5 4 3 2 1

A CIP catalogue record for this book is available from the British Library.

Designed by **Neal Townsend**
Printed by **Mackays of Chatham plc**

This book is dedicated to Matt Crawford, a true countryman with the word 'altruism' tattooed across his forehead, and also to the late Portia Antrobus, cruelly murdered by Phallustair Blandvoice and consigned to an early grave. We salute you both.

Disclaimer

Somewhere within the bowels of this book is a gratuitously offensive comment about people called Trevor. The author would like to say that while he would not wish to dissociate himself from this comment and indeed, having written it, he is hardly in a position so to do, he would nevertheless like to apologise to any large muscular Trevors with short fuses. Anyone else who has cause to be offended by the contents herein should be comforted by the knowledge that you can't make an omelette without breaking a few eggs.

Acknowledgements

The numerous hobby horses ridden with such enthusiasm by members of Archers Anarchists are brought into the world, fed and then kept on uncomfortable rubber matting at Christine's stables by more people than can be decently mentioned. Many similar theories about the truth in Ambridge are put forward with undoubted spontaneity by different people. The author wishes to thank all those Anarchists who take so much time and trouble to offer their thoughts and demonstrate an unstinting capacity to see it and tell it as it is.

From time to time we allude to *The Book of the Archers*, affectionately abbreviated to *BOA*. This is something of a BBC hagiography but, apart from containing some of the most castist photographs imaginable, it otherwise provides some useful semi-facts, including dates, upon which we have been able to base some of our revelations.

Contents

Introduction

This book could have fallen into your hands for a variety of reasons. Perhaps you were under the impression that the *Archers* bit referred to the ancient sport so effectively practised by Mr R. Hood and his somewhat dubious merry men. More likely your well-known zest for survival caused a well-meaning relative to buy it for you as a gift, in which case it will turn up in a charity shop quicker than a set of bath cubes.

But we are interested in listeners to BBC Radio 4's *The Archers*. Not just interested, but rather unhealthily obsessed in a crossing-over-to-the-other-side-of-the-road-when-you-see-us-approaching sort of way. There are several varied and valued categories of listener, including:

I've been listening since the end of Dick Barton – these listeners are by definition old. They clearly identify themselves as serious long-term players, although the way they refer to a kind of seamless continuity from the days of *Dick Barton 'Special Agent'* does sometimes make you wonder if they would have become just as attached to the shipping forecast if it had been put in the same time slot.

The wife listens to it so I can't help hearing it sometimes – these are the same people who collect autogaphs from celebrities explaining, 'It's not for me, it's for the boy.' They know every detail of the plot and will give themselves away within fifteen seconds of the beginning of the conversation by demonstrating the fact.

I have it on in the car sometimes – these are apologists. Like the previous type, they don't really want to admit that they are completely hooked because they feel there is something not quite decent about it. They are the type of people who, if you were to tell them that you did not possess a television, would hastily tell you that they only have a 'small black-and-white one', as if this demonstrated anything apart from general weirdness. Not only do they listen to *The Archers* in the car, but you can regularly see them in a supermarket car park having arrived at 7.08 p.m. sheepishly emerging from their vehicle at 7.15.

I only hear it occasionally but it doesn't seem to matter how many episodes you miss, you can always catch up – this is a comment frequently made about soaps and invariably accompanied by ladles of smugness. So far as *The Archers* is concerned it is palpably untrue. There are too many things that only occur once in a millennium in Ambridge and if you miss that crucial episode you will end up with a totally distorted view of the place. It is surprising, for example, just how many people believe that there are no cats in Ambridge. Yet sharper-eared and more diligent listeners will know that Ambridge is like a set for a feline version of *The 101 Dalmatians*. Indeed Sammy the Cat even speaks, which is more than can be said for half the characters.

If you listen to *The Archers* you are a good egg and all other personality flaws (homicidal tendencies etc.) can be forgiven, but Archers Anarchists are invariably people who have come out as fully fledged unapologetic listeners. We put in sixty-five hours a year, plus a few hours of repeats. We don't answer the phone during episodes and we don't accept social engagements before 7.15 p.m., but then we don't get invited to many so that helps a bit.

You may have read *The Archers Anarchists' A–Z*, a seminal work of encyclopaedic reference to some of the more interesting characters, animals and sites in Ambridge. This book is a different kettle of slurry. Mindful of the pressures that listening to *The Archers* can place on us all, we felt it would be helpful to examine in more detail some of the strange practices that pervade and the downright barking people who prowl the village. If you are to survive as an *Archers* listener you will need our help. The *Survival Guide* offers you as a reader and listener the opportunity to discover yourself (what a load of high-falutin' nonsense) from an *Archers* perspective. Not content merely to spew facts, we invite you to assess your own Archers-anarchic credentials, through our quizzes and questionnaires.

Archers Anarchists was born from a massive and nationwide revulsion to castism. Britain suffers from institutionalised castism and we devote a chapter to this canker. Sadly the Castism Awareness courses run by Archers Anarchists have done little to turn the tide. It is still all too common to hear people utter such obscenities as 'the actor who plays ****' and words like 'script' and 'cast' pepper the parlance of people who in their normal daily lives would not wish to hurt a fly.

The solution to this problem is not obvious. It requires a change in attitudes throughout the country. Castists tend to thrive in those areas where there is a greater density of Radio 4 listeners. The minority non-castist population can often feel itself patronised by those who pay lip service to anti-castism. They will say things like, 'Some of my best friends believe the Archers are real'. Yet the very use of the word 'believe' betrays a clear assumption on their own part that in fact *The Archers* are not real. You could just as easily substitute the words 'Father Christmas' for 'Archers' as far as they are concerned.

The other 'ism' against which we run a constant campaign is cosyism. The main perpetrators are members of the Archer clan, led by the dreadful smug duo of Shul-ugh Hebden-Blandvoice and Jill Foghorn Archer. When we tune in for our thirteen-minute fix towards the end of, or during, a hard day's work we expect a bit of rural blood and guts, not the radio equivalent of Posh Spice and David Beckham's wedding. In the good old days we were treated to such delights as the Ambridge Mail Van Robbery, such a successful heist that the Royal Mail has refused to enter Ambridge ever since. Sadly nowadays we have to endure the excitements of Usha Gupta and Roooooth the Geordie Whinger indulging in Salsa, whatever that may be.

We continue to wage war against the dreaded enemy Archers Anoraks, whose destructive commercial activities are still widely advertised by the state-owned BBC. It remains beyond comprehension to most of us that genuine *Archers* listeners are prepared to indulge in the fantasy that the living, breathing characters of Ambridge could be 'played' by a load of moth-eaten 'actors'.

Anyway, there's no point in an introduction really. Just get on and read it or recycle it (unless it's a library book). And thank you for buying it, you are helping to keep the wolf of castism from the door.

Glossary

Those who are unfamiliar with the affectionate names by which we know some of the characters might be confused. We have endeavoured to list below anyone who is generally known by another less appropriate name.

Angel of Death/Horrible Hayley	Hayley Jordan
Archers Anoraks	The 'official' fan club of *The Archers*
Damien Hebden-Blandvoice	Daniel Hebden
Foghorn	Jill Archer
Jailbird Carter	Susan Carter
One-eyed Monster/Cyclops	Mike Tugger (Tucker)
Peggoi	Peggy Woolley
Phallustair Blandvoice	Alastair Lloyd
Shul-ugh Hebden-Blandvoice	Shula Hebden-Lloyd
That Fisher Woman (TFW)	The Reverend Janet Fisher
Village Bicycle	Caroline Pemberton
Wiwyerm	William Grundy
Mrs High and Mighty	Jennifer Aldridge
Jeck	Jack Woolley

Aptitude Test
Are You an Archers Anarchist?

If you have never heard of Archers Anarchists you may be unsure whether or not you are one. This straightforward aptitude test generally proves 99 per cent reliable and saves on expensive visits to the shrink. Answer the following six questions and you will get an instant result.

1. When you hear a lovey-dovey scene with Shul-ugh and Phallustair Blandvoice which of the following most closely matches your thoughts?
a) 'Oh, how lovely. Don't they just make the most perfect couple?'
b) 'I do like Shula and Alastair but they are not terribly interesting.'
c) 'Give me legal immunity, a high-velocity rifle and the keys to Glebe Cottage and I'd have a field day.'

2. When young Damien Hebden-Blandvoice gives us the benefit of his velvet tonsils do you think:
a) 'What a sweet little boy. I could hug him. I'm so glad he has a nice new daddy.'

b) 'That's a rather unusual voice for a child.'

c) 'If this demonic little brat ever dives head first into a three-fathom slurry pit, I just hope his mother's there to enjoy it.'

3.Jailbird Carter is worried about her job and whether there's enough wonga coming into the Carter household to keep body and soul together. Is your reaction:

a) 'Poor Susan, she never has things easy coming from the dysfunctional Horrobin family. Can't the poor girl ever get a break in life?'

b) 'Susan – she's married to Neil, isn't she?'

c) 'Why doesn't she just go on the game?'

4.When Jill Foghorn Archer goes into manic cooking mode do you feel:

a) 'I can almost smell the delicious aromas emanating from her Aga.

b) 'Jill's one of the Ambridge stalwarts. When she dies, *The Archers* will die with her.'

c) 'Anyone who can pass up so many opportunities to put cyanide in her almond cakes isn't worth the time of day.'

5.When nice old Mrs Antrobus agreed to let her flat to Hayley Jordan, was your reaction:

a) 'Ah, it will be so nice for Hayley to have a base in the village once again and company for Mrs A.'

b) 'I'm not quite sure who Hayley is.'

c) 'Oh, my God, that's curtains for Mrs Antrobus, the Angel of Death's moving in.'

6.How did you react to the news that Elizabeth Pargetter is expecting twins?

a) 'That's lovely news. Just in time for the millennium. I think I'll start knitting a little present for them.'

b) 'Twins. Well, that will be interesting.'

c) 'Listening to nine months of that is going to be like having your fingers permanently wedged down your throat. I can't honestly see myself surviving.'

How did you score?

Mostly 'A's
You are definitely NOT an Archers Anarchist. You are probably a member of the 'official' fan club, Archers Anoraks, and you are one of the few remaining people on earth who still use tea cosies. You have listened to *The Archers* since *Dick Barton* went down the Swanee and you love all the goody-two-shoes characters. Fig rolls are only still on the market for your benefit. To save embarrassment all round, we would strongly recommend that you refrain from applying to join Archers Anarchists.

Mostly 'B's
You are well weird. You only listen to *The Archers* when there's a full moon and you have barely a clue what's going on. *The Archers* is certainly not in your blood (if you have any), and the only thing you've noticed about the world around you is that most people who come anywhere near you are armed with crosses and garlic.

Mostly 'C's
You are a truly excellent human being, imbued with an anarchic spirit and you recognise the people of Ambridge for what they are – ghastly. You will be totally at ease with everything we say and we want you to come round for tea to meet our mums.

A Breath of Fresh Air
Is Helen the Hazel of the New Millennium?

Anyone who challenges the cosy scone culture of Ambridge is to be embraced. The relatively recent arrival of Helen and her modern farming expertise gives rise to cautious optimism.

Helen Archer is one of the many characters who have managed to acquire an accent which is totally at odds with their origin and upbringing. Her childhood was spent in more or less total silence, yet even in her early teens she gave the occasional sign that she might turn out to be 'one of us'. Anyone who can break into Peggoi's cottage and turn it into a theatre of adolescent debauchery is worthy of our admiration.

After the death of Jaaaarn, Helen suddenly came out as a Sloane Ranger with a splendid 'OK-ya' voice. For the more long-in-the-tooth listeners who hanker after the lovely Hazel Woolley, Helen looks like she may well fill the void. One of the most striking similarities was the tendency for each to turn up, cause havoc and then depart from the scene. However, it seems that 'Helin' (as some people, including her mother, irritatingly call her) is becoming a rather more permanent fixture.

Before we discuss Helen's contribution to society we should just pause to regret that, due to her heavy work commitments,

Hazel was unable to attend Jeck's eightieth birthday celebrations. Despite being summoned by Peggoi, Hazel still took the reasonable view that whilst his funeral might be worth the journey, there was little point in showing up for a typical Archer Cosy-up where she would have been made to feel like a piece of excrement. Instead she sent a lovely card, twelve foot square, saying, 'Have a ball, hope it's a riot.' What more can you ask from an adoring stepdaughter?

A good indicator of just what an excellent person Helen can be is the fact that she doesn't 'see the point' of cricket. Presumably that is a state of mind shared by the Ambridge cricket team, which would go some way to explaining their results.

As someone who has never done a hand's turn in her life save for filling the odd yoghurt pot, Helen is admirably qualified to lecture her parents on marketing and brand image. She immediately saw that Brum Nanny Sausages were never going to be a real earner. And she consistently espoused the view that the organic pork industry would not be best served by someone whose day should be entirely taken up with the career of looking after other people's children.

To give Helen her due, something we are always pleased to do, she is one of those rare people in the village (the other is Brian) who actually want to see something run efficiently. Those who remember the estate office prior to the arrival of Hard-working Simon Pemberton (bless his cotton-enriched socks) will know that it was run like a holiday camp largely for the convenience of its staff. Shul-ugh and Jailbird Carter would spend all day making personal calls on the office phone, entertaining passers-by to coffee and a chat, and working the office photocopier round the clock to produce leaflets for all the busybody community groups in Borsetshire.

Similarly the dairy at Bridge Farm had become a repository

for the idle. Clarrie would turn up when it suited her, forgetting all the health and safety measures, and Tracy Horrobin would just not bother showing up at all. Helen recognised this and really tried to inject a bit of urgency and businesslike behaviour into the proceedings. Many profitable opportunities for the dairy have been squandered under the lax regime of Pat. For years Fat Clarrie has doubtless been gorging herself with churn-loads of cream on a 'one for me, one for the pot basis'.

It was Helen who saw what thousands of Anarchists knew Bridge Farm had been crying out for – a Hazard Analysis Critical Control Point Study. It was so blindingly obvious to most of us but no one but Helen had bothered to implement one. When she suggested this to Clarrie, it has to be said that Clarrie's response was embarrassing. She made the classic mistake of anyone who has a single-figure IQ of trying to be clever. When Helen patiently started to outline her systems and strategy for her HACCP (as we aficionados call it), Clarrie jeered 'Systems and strategy, eh? Let me guess, you learned about this at Reece Heath, didn't you?'

Clarrie is presumably the kind of person who walks into a doctor's surgery and when prescribed an antibiotic says 'Oh, I suppose you learned that at medical school, didn't you?' What we do have to remember about Clarrie is that it is for people like her that packets of salted peanuts are produced bearing the legend 'This product contains nuts.'

Helen is a real people's person, with an easygoing but efficient manner – the sort of person who would give you her last Rolo, and then send you a bill. Her efforts to introduce a training regime at the dairy were admirable. The extent to which Pat had allowed things to slide became apparent when Helen discovered an employee knocking around whom no one else ever seemed to have noticed.

Unfortunately 'Colin' was apparently more influenced by

Clarrie and therefore was sullen and resentful of Helen's efforts. As a former teacher he should have embraced the opportunity to learn and grabbed the chance with both hands. Alas, he was obviously the sort of teacher who thought that yoghurt pots were primarily intended as the raw materials of tedious infant sculptures rather than as receptacles for yoghurt.

It is a mystery how he came to be on the payroll of Bridge Farm without anyone realising, almost redolent of the ghost-workers in the pre-reconstructed newspaper industry. But Helen's real achievement was to enable the blossoming of Tracy Horrobin. She took to the new training like a duck to a Malteser (an interesting phenomenon if you are prepared to surrender a Malteser in the cause of science – children should be supervised).

The bitter feud between Fat Clarrie and Tracy served only to highlight all that is bad in Ambridge. Clarrie, having fought Helen tooth and nail, and poured scorn on all her training initiatives, expected that when Helen decided to create the much needed management function of assistant supervisor she would be first in line for the job. This despite the fact that she couldn't be bothered even to produce a simple flow diagram for Helen. Tracy on the other hand had recognised the old maxim 'If in doubt ask', and had enlisted the help of the MENSA-rated Jailbird to help her colour in a very attractive flow chart. Thus Tracy had demonstrated herself a willing and enthusiastic worker and eminently deserving of promotion – the first time a Horrobin had been promoted since the Am last froze over.

Fat Clarrie was outraged that Tracy had used her gumption and had been prepared to better herself. She duly tried to stitch her up, but luckily Helen had learned about people like Clarrie at Reece Heath in her Fat Employees With Attitude Problems classes. Clarrie was annoyed that Tracy, having become 'management', had the temerity to ask her to make a cup of tea.

But if you can't get your staff to make you a cuppa, what's the point of promotion?

Tracy fully justified Helen's faith in her by displaying an imaginative form of 'hands-off' management. Under Helen she was able to demonstrate her creativity, and almost immediately added a new flavour to the yoghurt range. Ash-flavoured yoghurt would have been a bestseller among all right-thinking non-PC people if only Tracy's genius had been properly recognised.

Helen really made an effort to persuade Clarrie to inculcate some basic standards of hygiene into the dairy routine. But it was a painfully uphill struggle. When it comes down to it, Clarrie is the kind of person whose ambition stretches no further than to be one of the people pulling moronic faces behind John McCririck on Channel 4 Racing. Helen's only management fault was that she did not immediately ask Clarrie to clear her desk. That task would have entailed nothing more than the removal of several forgotten items of decaying foodstuffs, a couple of Mills and Boons and one of those highly amusing postcards saying 'You don't have to be mad to work here but it helps.'

Lancastrian Tommy seems to have a bit of a problem with his sister's management style but this can be attributed to the more laid-back *'manyana'* way in which they work up north. He needs to learn that, for Southerners, efficiency comes somewhere between cleanliness and godliness. He also has to recognise the limitations of his own abilities, which are playing cricket, projecting diced carrot and running Roooooth a close second as international whingeing champion.

A firm believer in the family unit, Sloane Helen was justly outraged that Horrible Hayley continued to hang around like a bad smell long after Jaaaarn's death. So Helen's pointed references to Hayley as an outsider were quite befitting. After all, Hayley had had something of a hand in Jaaaarn's demise, having as good as told him he could stick his engagement ring through the nose of one of his pigs. There are those who think Helen is a trifle unpleasant, with her endless carping to Hayley about her not being part of the family, but sometimes the truth hurts and you have to be cruel to be cruel.

As the great sausage saga unfolded (you will find it well chronicled elsewhere in this book), Helen's perspicacity really came to the fore where Hayley was concerned. 'Am I the only one around here who can see what her game is? She's a gold digger, after a share in the farm.' The plain answer to her rhetorical question is that she was by no means the only person who could see through Hayley, you can add several hundred baying Anarchists. But it was comforting that Helen at least was not taken in.

Helen is by no means hard-hearted and many people must have warmed to her as she gently dealt with her mother's bout of sausage-induced depression, shouting at her in tones that put Foghorn in the shade and enthusiastically tipping Prozac down her throat.

One of the recurrent problems in *The Archers* is that some characters metamorphose into cosy goody-goodies. It was very alarming when Helen suddenly seemed to be under the misapprehension that she had made a bit of a horlicks of managing the dairy. She suddenly came over all tearful and Pat had to be taken out of her strait-jacket for an hour or so to 'sort it'. Then, having justifiably lambasted Lancastrian Tommy for his selfishness in dragging the noble name of Bridge Farm through the slurry, she suddenly admitted that she admired what he was doing. Helen should always remember that remorse is for softies.

Helen received little acclaim for her willingness to sacrifice her degree by helping out with the Bridge Farm shambles.

There are not many students who could find time to run a dairy while in the middle of a degree course. And in the face of all her adversity she still managed to walk off with the Reece Heath Prize for Business Student of the Year. So stick that one in yer yoghurt pot, Clarrie! Whether she will be able to get her hands permanently on the reins of power remains to be seen. Sadly, Pat's powers of recovery would suggest that the sloppy regime at Bridge Farm will continue for years to come.

One of our disappointments is that Helen has yet to devour the village menfolk. The only hint in this direction was mention of Trevor, the designer of acceptably modern yoghurt and sausage labels. It was quite obvious that Trevor's designs were well and truly set on Helen's King's Road knickers rather than yoghurt labels. But Trevor needs to learn that Sloane Rangers don't knock around with people called Trevor. In fact, does anyone?

If Helen is truly to emulate Hazel, and we desperately hope she will, then she needs to turn her attention to blokes who are to all intents and purposes in a happy relationship already. The problem is that most people in that category are already in her family, where divorce is unknown. But is that really a problem? It was once famously recommended that you should try anything once except folk-dancing and incest, so perhaps we could look forward to Helen seducing Tommy at a barn dance.

Tickle Your Taste Buds
A Selection of Culinary Delights from the Recipe Volumes of the Late Pru Forrest

Tibby Ta Ta

Preparation

Since the principal ingredient is Shul-ugh's cat, you will need to sneak into Glebe Cottage while the dreadful triumvirate are out in Borchester.

Ingredients
1 x Tibby
2 tbsp high-octane petrol
4lb red chillies
2 pints custard
Essence of Ippy

Fry Tibby in the petrol, reserving the tail. Remove any remaining fur. Add the chillies, custard and essence. Mix ingredients well and leave on a low Aga until Doomsday. Remove from heat just before serving. Use tail to garnish. Recommended wine to accompany: Blue Nun.

Cholesterol à la Clarrie
A favourite at Grange Farm.

Ingredients
2lb fresh lard
10 fl oz cooking oil
8 oz butter
5 tbsp turkey blubber
Dripping to season
10 oz pork scratchings
Feathers to garnish

Reserve the scratchings and feathers. Melt the other ingredients. Add the scratchings. Mix well. Refrigerate until set, then garnish with feathers. Serve with chips. As a variation for the diet-conscious, substitute 'I Can't Believe it's not Butter' for the butter.

Damien's Surprise
Very easy to make and very satisfying for the cook.

Ingredients
2 Cadbury's Creme Eggs
4 oz powdered glass
2 cups carpet tacks
8 tbsp bleach

Melt the eggs using an oxyacetylene blowtorch. Mix the ingredients together and put in an attractive jelly mould to set. Decorate with foxgloves and serve.

Roooooth's Steak and Kidney Pie

Preparation
A car journey to the cash and carry.

Ingredients
1 x Fray Bentos Steak and Kidney Pie

Open oven door, put pie in. Turn oven to 240° C/475° F/gas mark 9 and remove after half an hour's whingeing.
Note: Although Rooooth wouldn't, you may find it preferable to remove lid before cooking.

Kathy Perks's Hassett Room Delight

(Sorry – only joking. Did you really think Kathy would ever cook anything?)

Usha's Vegetarian Korma

Ingredients
Telephone
Phone Book

Dial the correct number for 'Star of Borchester' and order. Allow extremely long time for delivery as outsiders aren't really allowed into the village even when bearing takeaways.

Tractor Work
versus Manure

In recent times 'tractor work' has become the holy grail of all the Ambridge serfs. Eddie, Mike Tugger and Neil Carter line up each morning waiting to be hired for a day's 'tractor work' in order to put food on the tables of their respective families. Despite the number of farms in the area and the fact that no one ever seems to recruit new staff, the position never seems to get any easier and it is preordained that 'tractor work' will always be in scarce supply. It must be the hunger gnawing at their bellies that causes endless acrimony between the would-be tractor helmsmen as they fight for their prize. And, just to add spice to the contest, there now seems to be a new consolation prize – the right to vend and even spread manure.

Addiction to tractor work has taken on an almost spiritual dimension, and the late Jaaaarn must have become highly venerated for being able to die in the cab of his Fergie, or at least under it. The three main protagonists all feel they have an equal 'right to plough' and their respective wives act as village spin-doctors, trying to assert the claims of their husbands.

The person with the weakest claim is, of course, Eddie, who

has a whole farm of his own to run and only a near-octogenarian father to assist him. It is quite amazing that he spends his entire life looking for work without anyone saying to him, 'I'd have thought you'd have your work cut out at Grange Farm'.

Messrs Tugger and Carter have far more equal claims. Each has about a thousand joblets, some of them combined enterprises, and none of them seemingly yielding any income. The well-known 'curse of the Tuggers' determines that any venture upon which the One-Eyed Monster is embarked can only be modelled on the maiden voyage of the *Titanic*, whereas Neil's endeavours are always determined and toilsome but never fruitful.

Just to rub salt in the wound and in order to keep the proletariat where they belong, the organisation and allocation of tractor work is invariably handled with the utmost insensitivity. Despite the small scale of the local farms, even Home Farm, there always seems to be a mix-up whereby one of the three serfs is allocated work by, for instance Brian, unbeknown to Debbie, who has of course given the work to one of the others. This only causes more human misery since the person who is about to be disappointed, due to the cock-up, will, the previous night, have taken family and friends to Grey Gables to celebrate the awarding of the work. And so it will for ever continue. We hope.

Quiz One

IMPORTANT NOTE: *You should remember that this is an Archers Anarchist quiz and that the answers reflect the truth as we know it rather than the sanitised spin perpetrated by the BBC and the dreaded Archers Anoraks. We therefore suggest in some instances that marks should be deducted for having swallowed their propagandist line. This applies equally in the case of subsequent sections.*

Questions

1. What flavour were the prototype Brum Nanny sausages that caused such misery at Bridge Farm?
2. What was the make of tractor ridden by Jaaaarn Archer when he met his demise?
3. What caused the death of Phil's first wife?
4. What was the name of Hard-working Simon Pemberton's true love?
5. What crop, usually afflicted with some dire form of pestilence, does Neil Carter rely on to get his downtrodden family through the summer?
6. Who was the donor of Mountaineering Teddy?
7. Who was Dr Death's only named murder victim?
8. What is the most popular festival in the Ambridge social calendar?
9. What is the name of the beer most commonly drunk at the Bull?
10. What is the name of the competition at which a piece of imitation silverware is bitterly fought over annually by the village's cricketers?

Answers

1. Pork and leek.
2. Fergie (accept Fergusson).
3. Carelessness (accept flagrant abuse of fire regulations and health and safety legislation. Point deducted for 'She went to rescue a horse called Midnight from a burning Stable').
4. Mrs Harriet Williams (deduct point for cynical answer such as 'money').
5. Strawberries.
6. Hard-working Simon Pemberton.
7. Mrs Barraclough.
8. Diwali (accept Gay Pride March).
9. Shires.
10. Single Wicket Competition.

Don't Forget to Flush
Things That Never (or Rarely) Happen in Ambridge

While there can be no question that *The Archers* is anything other than real, it is nevertheless surprising that so many everyday things simply don't happen in Ambridge. Archers Anarchists can justly claim to have exerted some influence in these matters, for we find that certain things mysteriously occur for the first time when we point out their absence. It was with quiet satisfaction that we noted one of the first ever references to a television programme when Eddie admitted his previously well-hidden addiction to *Coronation Street*. That he should have chosen to watch a non-BBC soap was particularly laudable. Unfortunately, he seems to have forgotten his enthusiasm for 'Corrie' as he has never mentioned it again. Rare indeed are any references to children watching more than the occasional dose of televisual pap. This must be very satisfying to all the educationalists who tell us that 99 per cent of children watch TV for twenty-four hours a day.

Going into the Closet
Even the title of this chapter has been somewhat overtaken by events. When the BBC addresses some of these important

omissions from Ambridge life, the result tends to be rather like the fabled No. 9 bus – you wait forty-five years for someone to go to the lavatory and then suddenly everyone's permanently in the kasi. Until recently it was at least a habit confined to typically vulgar men, so imagine our shock and revulsion when Lynda Snell, blazing the trail for the women, suddenly announced she was off to 'powder her nose'. Dayveed was later described as being 'in the Gents' at the Cat and Fiddle, which could have set some tongues wagging in that particular watering hole.

Aerial Absence

Modern broadcasting devices such as satellite television have completely passed by Ambridge. More unusual is the complete absence of dreadful commercial music stations that so many people have as perpetual background to their work. You would expect the proletarian villagers, such as Jailbird, Clarrie, Eddie, Neil, Mike Tugger etc., to be inseparable from 'Wazzock FM' (broadcast twenty-four hours a day from Felpersham). Not that anyone usually listens to any form of radio; even Radio 4 is ignored by Mrs Antrobus, Foghorn, Phil, Peggoi and other likely listeners. Which leads us on to the perennial puzzle of why no one in Ambridge listens to *The Archers*. It is possible to envisage a wonderful scene where Foghorn is shouting away, clattering about in the kitchen at around 7.05 and is forced to complain that she can't hear herself shout above the noise of the radio featuring her shouting away. You get the picture? It would be tremendously helpful to the cause of anti-castism if, every so often, someone would say, 'I must get home to listen to *The Archers.*'

An isolated exception to all this emerged when Brian Aldridge was interviewed by Radio Borsetshire. Despite the station never having been mentioned before, it appeared that everyone had at least tuned in for his interview. Radio Borsetshire continued to be mentioned for a while until the inhabitants of Ambridge forgot about it. We have to give the station credit. The standard of interviewing of poor Brian was quite Paxmanesque and he received much more of a grilling than is normal in the anodyne fare common to most local radio. That having been said, it then hit rock bottom with a ludicrous set of interviews with Neil and Horrible Hayley on the riveting subject of strawberries. Fortunately the Ambridge Thought Police soon realised people were receiving signals from outside the village and the station was rapidly scrambled. If you now attempt to tune in you will find the Tommy Croker Quartet playing military music twenty-four hours a day.

No News is No News

Until recently there was no apparent means of obtaining newspapers in the village, with the obvious exception of the *Borchester Echo*. This presented no immediate problems as no one ever seemed to want to read one. But in 1999, Robert Snell broke all the rules in the book by going into the village shop to buy his Sunday papers.

This was an amazing feat, because there has never previously been any mention of the shop being open on a Sunday. Surely we would have heard *ad nauseam* if Beddy Tugger or Jailbird were being expected to work Sundays and Jeck would have been making his constipated firm managerial noises all over the place. Not content with just buying a paper in a one-off aberration, Robert proceeded to buy a newspaper for the following few Sundays and it seemed to have become something of a fixation with him. He simply couldn't stop talking about how much he was looking forward to reading them. So severe was his addiction and so infectious that even the illiterate Fat Clarrie started buying a tabloid, presumably for the pictures. Local media moguls were obviously impressed with the new zest for news in Ambridge because out of nowhere suddenly appeared the *Felpersham Advertiser*. As with radio, the news blackout was soon imposed and Sunday papers are once again reserved as an occasional treat.

I T or E T?

But then Robert Snell is the token person to have contact with the outside world. In most villages nowadays there are more people with computer expertise than Foghorn has cooked hot dinners. But in Ambridge there is just narrowly more than Roooooth or Usha has *cooked* hot dinners – namely Robert. He is referred to in hushed (apart from by Foghorn) and revered tones for his infinite technological wisdom. To be fair, computers have crept into the village, but they still tend to be referred to as items of some rarity – witness the hoo-ha when Joan Pargetter wished to borrow the only computer at Lower Loxley to write her novel. Robert is also the only person in the village to own a camera, but at least it's a digital one.

Where are the Toffs?

One of the most glaring deficiencies in Ambridge nowadays is that there are virtually no 'County' people. In the good old days we had the Fairbrothers, the Lawson-Hopes, Brigadier Winstanley, Ralph Bellamy, Lady Isobel Lander and the Tregorrans, to name but a few. Now all we have left in the village are the middle and lower classes. The Village Bicycle is County but her uncle, Lord Netherbourne, is not an Ambridge person. We are sometimes meant to believe that the silent Sir Sidney and Mercedes Goodman are County types. But they are more in the new-money mould of Jeck Woolley and probably made their dosh from scrap metal, with Sidney getting his knighthood for donations to Harold Wilson in the early 1970s.

Woeful Welfare

The Social Services are completely absent from Ambridge, particularly surprising given the number of wayward children and the apparently grinding poverty that afflicts so many of the characters. It was only in early 1999 that we learned of 'all the staff' at the doctor's surgery – presumably a silent army of nurses on permanent standby to remove the nits from the hair of the Grundy boys and Christopher 'Elephant Man' Carter.

Throw away the Key

Another thing that seems to be absent from Borsetshire in general is the release of prisoners. At the time of writing it is several years since Spanner and Craven were jailed for mistaking Usha Gupta's letter box for a sewage treatment works. Since we now live in the touchy-feely world where murderers are let out of prison after a year or so with an apple, a balloon and a going-home present, it seems extraordinary that these people have languished for so long at Her Majesty's pleasure. In fact, Her Majesty must be becoming rather bored with their company. Similarly we might have expected to see Clive Horrobin back in the bosom of his family before now.

Wheelie Strange

There are some very mundane absentees and one such example concerns refuse collection. No one ever puts their bin out. Indeed the thorny and sensitive issue of whether they have wheelie-bins has never so much as surfaced. Yet wheelie-bins have rent in twain many a community. Surely, from time to time we should be able to witness a snarl-up in the farmyard at Brookfield or Home Farm as the dustcart attempts to manoeuvre itself, accompanied by the silent barking of excited farm dogs. It should perhaps be acknowledged that Foghorn did allegedly inform the newly arrived Siobhan Hathaway of the day that the bin men came, but since we never hear them perhaps she was just relating a historical event.

Till Death Us Do Part?

Divorce is not quite an unknown phenomenon in Ambridge but contestants for the Dunmow Flitch could fill several coaches. The divorce rate is way below the national average and in the few cases where anyone is divorced it tends to have happened before the arrival of the character in the village. Robert Snell divorced the ludicrously named Bobo long before he married Lynda and moved to the village. Kathy Perks's first husband, Steve, breezed into the village momentarily but it was all done and dusted without him staying. Boring George Barford was already divorced when he arrived, as were Phallustair Blandvoice (or so he says, we see it differently) and Robin Stokes.

The strangest feature is that the trend in Ambridge is completely different from that in the rest of the country in that there is actually a decline in the divorce rate. In the past we at least had Mrs High and Mighty Aldridge divorcing Roger the Dodger, a man who never received due acclaim for murdering Handbag Hebden. Greg Salt, a kind of prototype Mike Tugger divorced Nora, who eventually shacked up with Boring George. And, of course, dear old Jeck Woolley divorced Valerie.

'The Appeared'

Perhaps the most intriguing and sinister absence is that of anyone's past, with the exception obviously of the indigenous population. A fair number of new characters have arrived in the village over a period of time but virtually no one brings much of a past with them. When you pause to consider some of our bastions of Ambridge life, we know very little about whence they came. Brian Aldridge turned up around 1975 loaded with wonga to the extent that he could buy a farm but never has any relation of his come to visit him nor has he ever visited them.

Similarly Sid – you might have thought that some of his old criminal mates would call by to chat about the good old days. Pat had her Uncle Haydn, who preceded her to Ambridge, but could not a few other relations find time to prise themselves away from their sheep to see her occasionally? The Snells are not the most exciting people in the world, but wouldn't there be the occasional Sunningdalese visitor or wouldn't Lynda want to go back to tell all her old neighbours what a mark she has made in her new area? Neil Carter had relatives back home when he first arrived in the village but he seems to have forgotten them. Phallustair, of course, has no visitors but we explain this elsewhere in this book. Since there has to be an irritating exception to every rule, Horrible Hayley brought her silent grandparents to the village to be photographed guzzling wine and eating strawberries. In fact we were probably witness to the first silent drunken grandma on British radio.

Even those who do have relatives only seem to have them on a temporary basis, perhaps when they first arrive, and then they cease to exist. We had the occasional visit from Terry Boring-Barford, who had inherited every bit of his father's boringness with some to spare, but that was long ago and daughter Karen has never appeared. Dr Death had no relations, but he'd probably disposed of them. Even St Usha can only muster two relations.

Anarchists have long discussed the vexed subject of 'the disappeared' but perhaps we have neglected to point out that there must be many people in Ambridge who *are* 'The Disappeared' to their own relations. Somewhere in some far forgotten corner of England there is an old withered Aldridge. Tied to an unpruned tree is a yellow ribbon, blowing pathetically and forlornly in the breeze.

Housebuyers' Heaven

Not all the things missing from Ambridge are to be regretted, and the arrival of Smarmball Doctor Tim and his Missus indicated one of the benefits of living in this particular village. Many frustrated house-buyers and sellers were green with envy at the speed with which the Hathaways were able to view 'The Cottage formerly known as Honeysuckle', sell their own property, carry out the surveys and move in, all in just four weeks. Most of us find that it takes about that time to get an estate agent or solicitor to return our calls but in Ambridge it is Nirvana.

And it didn't stop there. Naturally the cottage did not have adequate space to accommodate the doctor's enormous bedside manner and so an early extension was essential. Since the demise of SDP councillor Handbag Hebden, whose political party seemed to go the same way as him, there has been no form of local government in Borsetshire apart from the parish council. Thus it would appear that it is a complete haven from any kind of planning regulation since Token Brumvoice Jason was constructing one of his famous extension-cum-demolitions before you could say Planning Consent.

Break Away?

The song 'We're All Going on a Summer Holiday' is more or less taboo in Ambridge. Certainly holidays are not unknown, but they are very few and far between. In the rest of the country most people with an average or higher income can be expected to have one or two holidays during the year. But it would seem that you can only expect a holiday once every few years if you live in Ambridge and it is unusual for more than one person or family to be away at the same time. People don't even go away for short breaks. Even the well-to-do such as Jeck and Peggoi, Brian and Jennifer and Bicycle Pemberton don't seem to manage a holiday every year.

Ironically, or perhaps inevitably, when someone does have a holiday it is likely to be a big one and will be the talk of the village, e.g. Foghorn and Phil on the occasional trip to see wastrel son Kenton, or Usha and TFW on their dreadful walking holiday. The other feature of holidays when they do happen is that they are invariably taken with the utmost reluctance. Someone will always fight tooth and nail against the idea, either on grounds of cost or because 'there's far too much to do on the farm'.

Clarrie manages the occasional trip to Meyruelle, although people in Ambridge forget about their twinning arrangements for years at a time. It is rather painful hearing her struggle with her French and we can't help feeling she would be more comfortable with an annual week in Torremolinos, where she could get a decent piece of battered cod and chips with a nice lard dressing.

Sport in Question

It takes a great deal to get anyone in Ambridge interested in sporting events apart from those that occur within the village. There can be no other corner of the British Isles where boules is discussed more frequently than football with a reference ratio of about 60:1. The *BOA* tries to deny this by describing one or two people's alleged enthusiasms but this only makes the situation more absurd. For example, Roy Tugger is described as 'crazy about Aston Villa FC', yet he has barely been heard to mention football at all. Aston Villa, as the local Premiership club to Ambridge, gets to be discussed about once every couple of years, such as the occasion when the Grundys went there at Christmas 1997. In the 1998/99 season Villa went from top of the league to a losing run of nine or ten games – quite a reversal of fortunes in anyone's book – but the 'crazy' Tugger lad was apparently unmoved.

The usual pub bar conversation of a Saturday night when the afternoon's footie results are dissected piece by piece just never takes place. In the World Cup there were one or two references to the competition but never to the results. No one ever backs the winner in the Grand National and until the Boat Race is relocated to the Am it doesn't look like we're going to hear anything about that either.

There was, however, a single and rather peculiar reference to the Cricket World Cup in summer 1999. It was mentioned that failed ex-feed rep Neil Carter had been given a ticket to the semi-final in Edgbaston by one of his old customers. It is an extremely unlikely form of corporate hospitality where someone decides to bestow such favours upon junior former employees of their suppliers rather than their own customers, but such is Borchester life.

Wimbledon got a couple of mentions in 1999. Unfortunately Foghorn stayed in to watch it on television on a day when it was completely rained off, but she didn't seem to notice – probably sat there quite happily without even switching the TV on. People from Ambridge never go to Ascot or Henley, which is just as well as the Anarchist HQ is in Henley and we would be most upset to bump into any of them.

Grunge Farm
The Rehabilitation of the Grundys

It is a well-documented phenomenon that age tends to mellow people and, with a few honourable exceptions, former revolutionaries tend to become establishment pussycats. Sadly, this has happened to the Grundies in a big way. For those listeners who can recall the days of Dastardly Dan, there will be strong memories of the constant vilification of the Grundys by the Archer establishment. No one ever had a good word to say to a Grundy and voices would immediately intone with rank hostility the moment Joe or Eddie joined a conversation. In those days the question, 'What are you doing here?' would literally be spat, though perhaps with less frequency than we have to bear today. Grundys were lazy slackers, poachers and n'er-do-wells. The only exception was the silent Susan Grundy, who was a typical Ambridge cooking guru – a kind of Foghorn on Mogodon.

Anarchists would have loved the Grundys of yesteryear. Any enemy of an Archer is always a friend of ours. But tragically and for no accountable reason, people over the years have started being nice to them. There is no justification – Joe is still a foul-mouthed old goat, Eddie is still a poacher and they all still whinge on ceaselessly as if the world owes them a living. Their children are both suitably weird. You have Wiwyerm, who would rather rear pheasants than get a good crop of GCSEs, and Edward, who is a bit of a pansy – painting eggs when he should be going round looking for smaller children to bully. Clarrie's voice is just too ridiculous for us to waste any sympathy in her direction.

A major turning point in attitudes to the Grundys occurred when Hard-working Simon Pemberton sensibly decided that Grunge Farm would be better suited to a major flax plantation than a scrap metal and turkey yard. He rightly gave them notice to quit and Wiwyerm helpfully set light to the place by dropping a lighted fag end, resulting in a particularly hot dog. All of a sudden people in the village came rallying to their defence. The likes of Dayveed were to be heard calling Eddie 'mate' and the awful Shul-ugh was going out of her way to help them with their insurance claims. This of course was another criminal conspiracy because an insurance company would not expect to be paying out on damage caused by arson on the part of one of the beneficiaries from the claim. The one person who didn't lift a finger to help was Jailbird Carter, who knows a bunch of wasters when she sees them.

Jailbird had for once in her life acted like a loyal employee, remaining absolutely shtum when Fat Clarrie kept asking her why the insurance hadn't come through. Clarrie tried the old blackmail trick of, 'Oi thort we was meant to be best friends,' and unfortunately Jailbird turned turtle and rather belatedly let her in on the flax plans.

There is no proper explanation as to why the Grundys are and always have been totally penniless. They are tenant farmers, employ no staff and have a complete monopoly on turkey production, breeding a unique kind of silent, gobble-free turkey. At any given time Fat Clarrie has approximately five full-time jobs albeit of a staggeringly menial nature. It is hard to imagine that Grunge Farm produces anything at all since no one seems to work it. Eddie will do any other kind of work, however lowly, rather than farm his own land. He regularly lines up with all the other hired hands seeking 'tractor work'.

Statistically, if you devote your life to inventing illegal or semi-legal scams, some of them are going to work, yet everything touched by a Grundy goes belly-up.

Although it is rarely mentioned, Edward is raking it in as a castrato, singing in illicit concerts all round the world, hence the reason we haven't heard him in Ambridge since he sang at the 1995 Ambridge carol service, live from Westminster Abbey.

Wiwyerm has become a nasty case of poacher turned fascist as he marches round the covers in the Country Park threatening to shoot people's dogs. If he was a real old-style Grundy he'd shoot the dogs without asking questions first and would turn up at Grunge Farm with a few brace of pheasant for his dad to sell. Perhaps we are speaking too soon, for he has time on his side. Even Gregarious Greg Turner, who initially had the good sense to pour scorn on the idea of employing offspring from one of Borsetshire's leading criminal fraternities, is now reduced to fawning adoration of Wiwyerm's every step. Wiwyerm has done several ridiculous things that are anathema to the Grundys of yesteryear, notably selling Posh Spice to pay off his parents' debts, and paying his keep. Where will it end? Will he be taking holy orders when he should be nicking from the collection plate?

The Grundys who vacillate between dishonesty and stupidity, have become an embarrassment. Nowadays they are regarded as lovable rogues and the moment anyone becomes lovable they lose our support. We could badly do with Wiwyerm lighting up again and they can all go out in a blaze of glory.

Braveheart
Jamie Perks

For some unaccountable reason Archers Anarchists have occasionally been accused of negativity. 'Is there no one for whom you have a good word?' whimpers the occasional faintheart as they hastily try to conceal their Archers Anoraks membership card. We have just two words to stop them in their tracks – they are 'Jamie' and 'Perks', consecutively, contiguously and with profound respect.

There is no doubt that Jamie will become a great man. We are all familiar with those people in life for whom, in their formative years, the bread lands butter-side down on so many occasions that there seems no alternative but to stop buttering bread completely. Yet miraculously they reappear poking their defiant heads above the brown stuff. Such a sprog is Jamie Perks.

We have to admit culpability in neglecting Jamie. We completely overlooked him in our *A–Z*, didn't even give the little blighter a couple of lines. Yet just consider what he has had to contend with.

Firstly he was born a Perks. No one is really called Perks – at least there are only three in the Reading phone book, hopefully three rather small, passive Perkses. His mother rejected him before he was even born. She was going around the village refusing to discuss her pregnancy and for a while the mere mention of 'baby' within earshot of Kathy drew the same response as saying 'Sausages' to Pat. She vaguely warmed to the idea of being a mother as time went on, largely because she realised that it would give her at least a temporary excuse to keep away from serving in the Bull and all those dreadful customers. You can never underestimate what Kathy will do to avoid cooking and the catering business – she even lent her saucepans to the depressingly one-dimensional Siobhan.

His next problem was being given a perfectly good traditional name like James and having it automatically converted to the OK-ya version of 'Jamie'. On the rare occasions he is allowed to mix with other children they must really tease him about his cut-glass silent accent and his Sloany name. The thing that parents don't realise when they name their children is how ridiculous those names will sound when the child grows up. Even Kate twigged this one when she eventually decided against calling her child 'Baby'.

Jamie has never been permitted to see his half-sister, Lucy, because she is one of 'The Disappeared'. For several years he was apparently kept in some kind of cage, possibly with Eccles the peacock, since his sunny silent tones were never heard in the Bull and only recently does anyone talk to him. We are virtually certain that he has been brought up to all intents and purposes as a peacock. But the good thing about Jamie is that he doesn't let little things like this get him down. And all of a sudden he showed the mettle of a true champion at the noble art of egg-rolling.

What marked Jamie out as a true braveheart was not so much the mere fact of winning in this rather absurd sport but that he was prepared to take on all the forces of evil ranged against him in the person of the awful Damien. While that dreaded possessed child had his black heart set on victory, Jamie fearlessly showed that the forces of good are still alive in Ambridge.

But realistically, though we admire him, Jamie is perhaps foolhardy. You don't cross the Archer Mafia and live to tell the tale, and no one can honestly fancy his chances in later life against the darker forces of Damien. You will not have to wait too long before hearing, 'It was a complete accident – Jamie and Daniel were just playing together when Jamie fell into the Am. Daniel tried to rescue him but apparently the game they were playing involved Jamie having a large quantity of house bricks in his pocket and a lump of concrete tied to his leg.' In the meantime he fights back against all the odds. Often left in the care of the Angel of Death, Horrible Hayley, he rarely squeaks out but accepts life's lot. He has a voice of sorts that emerges on saints' days and other festivals but it is 95 per cent peacock, five per cent human.

In recent times Jamie has been known to mix with those strange creatures Peeeep and BSE Josh, produced by the ghastly Rooooth. In turn this led him to encounter Heather and her appalling husband, Solly. But the excellent Jamie was having none of this charade and downright refused to speak to Heather. Cursed he may be, but we love him.

From the Cutting-room Floor I
The Arrival of the First Mrs Blandvoice

Archers Anarchist militants have broken into the BBC strong-room and obtained some dialogue which is currently being withheld from adoring listeners. It concerns the vital matter of the first Mrs Blandvoice. Listeners will well remember how Phallustair suddenly refused to have a church wedding with the awful Shul-ugh when he realised that he was going to have to discuss his first marriage in a no-holds-barred session with That Fisher Woman. Wrongly, many people assumed he just could not 'bear to bare' his soul to a woman who is so clearly a theological impostor. But the truth was far more interesting. The following transcript liberated from the cutting-room floor makes fascinating reading.

The scene is the village shop on a summer afternoon. Beddy Tugger and Jailbird Carter are quietly pilfering stamps, falsifying child benefit claims and engaging in desultory conversation.

Beddy: At least Mike's getting some tractor work. Oh, sorry Susan, I didn't mean ...

Jailbird: Oh, that's all right, Betty, Neil's quite enjoying clearing dogs' mess from the village green. He doesn't need tractor work.

Shop bell rings and a woman in her thirties enters, complete with horribly disfigured face.

Beddy: What brings you here?

Jailbird: Yeah, what the f*** do you think you're doing – a member of the public coming into a shop?

Quasimodette: Well, actually, it's awfully nice of you to ask but I didn't come in to buy anything. I'm looking for the home of someone called Phallustair Blandvoice-acid-thrower.

Jailbird: Do you mean Shul-ugh's husband?

Quasimodette: No, he can't be anyone's husband, he's still married to me.

Jailbird: But we've got a Phallustair Blandvoice here in Ambridge. He's the vet.

Quasimodette: Oh, no, he's not pretending to be a vet again, is he?

Beddy: (*gulping*) Pretending?

Quasimodette: I'm afraid Phallustair is a very sick man. He spent ten years in prison after eating two of our children.

Jailbird: (*with enthusiasm*) Oh, that's nice, I've been in prison, too. We can have a good old natter about it.

Quasimodette: While he was in prison he started reading one or two books about veterinary science and when he was let out he immediately set himself up as a vet. He's got no qualifications at all.

Jailbird: (*proudly*) I haven't got any qualifications.

Beddy: (*with a voice resonant of a monkfish choking on a Brillo pad*) So, did he come back to you after leaving prison?

Quasimodette: Oh, he came back to me all right, just long enough to redesign my face in an acid attack. I went to the police, but they let him off with a caution as long as he went to live somewhere off their beat. I haven't seen him again, though he still sends cards to the children.

Beddy: But I thought you said he ate the children?

Quasimodette: No, I'm talking about the other five. Sorry, we haven't really introduced ourselves, have we. I'm Quasimodette Blandvoice.

Jailbird: Very pleased to meet you. You remind me of my Christopher.

Exit Quasimodette.

Jailbird: What was I saying? Oh, yes, tractor work.

The Great Sausage Betrayal
From Pork to Prozac

> 'Those blessed sausages, they've caused so
> much strife in this family.'
> **Pat Archer, 8 March 1999**

Spring 1999 was largely devoted to one of the most riveting plots ever to be served up on the airwaves. The degree of acrimony arising from this situation was sufficient to send poor Pat from Bridge Farm to Funny Farm. It all stemmed from the somewhat deranged plan of Horrible Hayley and Lancastrian Tommy to produce organic sausages. Everyone accepts that there are a number of risks associated with allowing a team headed up by a serial poisoner to go into food production, yet strangely this never actually came into the equation.

There was an early hiccup in the whole enterprise when Hayley, with all the relevant experience that comes from looking after toddlers, excitedly told Tommy how they would be able to produce 'different kinds' of sausages. A completely nonplussed Tommy asked, 'What do you mean?' and Hayley had to break it to him that sausages were not actually grown from seeds – they could, in fact, be subject to variations in ingredients, thus resulting in different flavours. Once over this little hurdle it looked as if they'd be laughing all the way to the abattoir, but sadly it was not to be.

Initially Tony and Pat were as enthusiastic as two terminally miserable people can be, but it was the intervention of the excellent Helen that turned the tide. Helen managed to persuade her parents that if the sausages were to be marketed without a newly revamped Bridge Farm label then a great plague and pestilence would fall upon the farm. We can only assume that with the death of Jaaaarn still fresh in their minds they just didn't want to take the risk. For although we have nothing but respect for Helen's marketing expertise, it is not immediately apparent that the labelling of sausages is that important. It is not unusual for sausages to be sold loose, in which case they wouldn't have a label at all.

Much to the chagrin of Britain's most unlikely coupling of entrepreneurs, Pat and Tony pulled the plug on the whole venture at Helen's insistence and refused to fund it.

Ambridge may lack many of the facilities and services available in most medium-sized villages but one thing it does have is a resident venture-capitalist. Indeed, there is hardly a person below the age of thirty in the Archer family who is not up to their eyeballs in debt to Peggoi Woolley. Hayley and Tommy went hot-foot to Peggoi to see if she would stump up the readies. Peggoi, always partial to the occasional sausage, was only too pleased to get involved initially. But not having the blessing of Pat and Tony turned out to be like having a bad reference from a credit-checking company, and when Peggoi learned that these sausages were to be produced without a state-of-the-art label she immediately changed her tune.

Desperate, Hayley and Tommy considered other ways of raising the capital. They overlooked the obvious solution, which was to steal from poor old blind Mrs Antrobus, but this was presumably because Hayley regarded Mrs A as a long-term investment. Ironically the modest funding eventually came from the most unpredictable of sources, the very people who had withdrawn it in first place. When it came to Tommy's birthday (and what a jolly affair that was!) Pat, despite having talked of nothing else for the previous month, had not been able to think of anything to get him for a present and therefore wrote out a cheque, thus inadvertently solving the Brum Nanny Sausages cash-flow problem.

The subterfuge had only just begun. Cash duly secured, the next problem was that, for some reason best known to himself, the butcher who would construct the sausages required the leeks ready-chopped. Preparing leeks at Bridge Farm would have been akin to setting up a charcuterie in a synagogue and, by a cruel twist of fate, Hayley did not seem to have a sink in her flat at Nightingale Farm. This meant that an accomplice was needed in this vicious plot. Step forward Jailbird Carter. Well used to harbouring criminals, the temporary loan of a sink was chicken-feed to her and she even helped in the dirty deed.

The next obstacle in the whole ghastly business was that when Hayley and Tommy were about to set off, armed to the teeth with pigs and leeks, Pat suddenly decided that a trip to the abattoir was her ideal day out. They only managed to deter her by gently convincing her that she was completely bonkers.

The denouement came with the triumphal arrival of Lancastrian Tommy back at Bridge Farm accompanied by 50 lb of organic pork and leek sausages. Having gone to inordinate lengths to produce these comestibles in the utmost secrecy, it was rather bewildering that he was so quick to flaunt them before the unstable Pat, particularly bearing in mind her deep-seated sausage phobia.

On cue, Pat completely trolleyed it on sight of the offending sausages. 'Get out of my sight,' she said to her errant son. It's difficult and inappropriate for us to make a value judgement and the jury could go either way in determining the sanity of an eighteen-year-old who chooses 50 lb of sausages as his coming-of-age present.

But that was by no means the end of the matter as Helen, by now famous for her numerous unannounced appearances when everyone thought she was meant to be at college, suddenly showed up. Her antennae had picked up the word 'sausages' and she launched a complete rocket attack on the whole project. Hayley was suddenly cornered like a rat and her veneer of syrup fell away as she lashed out at Helen, accusing her of all things under the sun. Pat was forced to retreat to her boudoir with a touch of the vapours.

It further transpired that the leeks were, of course, stolen from Pat and Tony, a crime for which hanging would be akin to a total reprieve. Needless to say, Brum Nanny sausages were eagerly snapped up by the odd but appreciative Borsetshire public. Never mind the problems of rural transport, people were travelling from miles around, turning up at Bridge Farm at all hours of the day to get half a pound of the contentious bangers.

But Pat and Tony were adamant. No matter how many millions of sausages were sold, if they didn't have one of Trevor's as yet unproduced labels, they were illegal. Pat was actually confined to her bed for at least two weeks, suffering from the constant pressure to permit the illicit production to continue. It can't have helped matters that, during this time, Foghorn would appear on the hour every hour to attempt to pour soup down her throat, while the insensitive Tommy wanted to revive her with a constant regime of bangers and mash. It became like a slapstick 'Don't mention the war' routine. Nobody seemed capable of talking to Pat for more than about twenty seconds without mentioning sausages and this would immediately cause a relapse. For weeks, Pat could be reduced to tears by the mere mention of the 'S' word.

Perhaps the most amazing incident in the whole débâcle occurred at 7.15 p.m. on Sunday, 21 March 1999. Lancastrian Tommy, suffering from a kind of reverse syndrome to his mother's whereby he could think of nothing but sausages, suddenly declared that the attitude to Hayley over the whole business 'is really pissing me off'.

The nation stood stock still. Sunday roasts being taken from their respective ovens went crashing to the floor. Those roasts in a more advanced stage of the cycle lodged in their eaters' throats. Birds stopped singing. After forty-eight piss-free years and despite the numerous provocations during that time – armed robberies, murders, outbreaks of foot-and-mouth disease, TB etc., etc., it took a few pounds of pork and leek sausages to trigger off the first ever piss in Ambridge. Whether anyone in the village noticed is open to conjecture. The signature tune hastily cut in the moment the word was uttered, and by Monday we can only assume that all villagers in the know had been sworn to secrecy.

Things went from bad to worse at Bridge Farm. Pat was by now a mere step away from Château Insane as she seemed unable to recover from the whole sausage ordeal. For someone with such a generally short fuse, Tony had played a blinder and taken on the role of mediator with relish for the task. Thanks to Helen's tip-off, he had stepped in to ensure that Horrible Hayley would not become a partner in the burgeoning sausage empire. Hayley had sufficiently poisoned the mind of Lancastrian Tommy to ensure that he was going to go round like he'd lost a fiver and found a euro for some time to come. It was noticeable that for several weeks around this time, he was permanently off his food. It is a wonder he was not treated for anorexia.

One day towards the end of March, the deranged Pat suddenly turned on poor Tony and accused him of being hard on Tommy and a 'bad manager'. Not content to stop there, she went on to say that this was exactly how he had treated Jaaaarn. Tony was stung to the quick and suddenly adopted a strangulated voice like that of Charlie Drake singing 'My Boomerang Won't Come Back', asking, 'You're not blaming me for John's death, are you?' But, oh yes, she was, and there was no stopping her. All of a sudden we thought we were in heart-attack territory as Pat, like a wailing banshee, came over all unnecessary.

Poor Tony was so shaken by the whole business that he couldn't remember the number 999 to call an ambulance. Totally overcome by the all-pervading demonic influence in the village he kept dialling 666. And there we were left at 7.15 p.m. on a Friday night with a good old-fashioned cliff-hanger, wondering whether by Sunday night Horrible Hayley would be busy writing poetry and TFW would be getting ready for more pagan festivities.

But, alas, this was the cruel 1990s and by Sunday Pat was back to being quietly doolally in her bedroom with the curtains closed. Apparently it was nothing more than a bit of sausage-induced hyperventilation. Tony seemed to have forgotten that he was currently standing accused of murder and merrily suggested to Pat that she may feel better if they took a trip to look at Brian Aldridge's top-security genetic research establishment. There's nothing like a double-headed sheep or a field of talking barley to make you feel better when you've been hyperventilating.

Eventually, someone decided that as Pat had spent the previous six weeks in bed and was rapidly becoming like a walk-on part in *One Flew Over the Cuckoo's Nest* it might be worth getting the doctor in. The BMA have an agreement that all doctors in Ambridge will be great ambassadors for the profession, so we can only assume that they must have had a brief falling out with the BBC during the time Dr Death was there. Dr Tim is back in the groove as an all-round nauseatingly good guy who dispenses bucketloads of sympathy whether or not it is requested or deserved.

Despite the fact that Dr Death had apparently neglected to mention in Pat's medical notes the small matter of her losing her son, Dr Tim was soon on the case. Within minutes he had set Pat well on the road to being our first Ambridge junkie.

After her huge fracas with the Bridge Farm gang, Horrible Hayley was completely gob-smacked by the revelation that Pat might be suffering from 'depression'. Her reaction was, 'I can't believe it.' What the million or so listeners couldn't believe was that she should be so surprised that Pat should be depressed by having an East End-style gangland war fought out in her farmyard – over pork and leek sausages.

Thankfully, marketing guru Sloane Helen got her way and the sausages were duly given their labels, emblazoned with the name that had advertising agencies dropping their collective jaws with admiration, 'Bridge Farm Organic Sausages'. Unfortunately, the very appearance of these labels led Tommy to go off the deep end in a manner not seen since his gracious appreciation of his eighteenth-birthday celebrations.

As the weeks wore on, the whole subject of sausages was reduced to the status of an unstable semi-dormant volcano. At Helen's birthday party it was actually Pat who mentioned the war with a, 'How are the sausages coming on, Tommy?' The nation held its breath, but there was no need to worry because this was False Jollity Awareness Day at Bridge Farm and fuses were to stay in tact. In fact the only enduring memory from Helen's festivities was the revelation that Pat is tone deaf and cannot sing in tune. Her rendition of 'Happy Birthday' will linger in our ears for far too long.

Anyone who thought that Pat was cured was in for a bitter disappointment. When they get hold of a new idea, they hang on to it for grim death. And, after all, the idea of someone going around Ambridge like a permanent wet weekend was so novel, you could hardly blame them for milking it a bit. Much to the chagrin of the pharmaceutical industry, the happy pills that Pat was eventually forced to take did not have an instantaneous effect. But then, if the rest of us had sons with the temerity to set up a small-scale sausage-making enterprise, we would all doubtless find that it needed more than a few milligrams of Pfizer's finest to set us back on the straight and narrow.

When the drugs had failed there was urgent consultation over what steps to take next. It was felt that Pat needed to talk to someone who might understand what she was going through, a task probably best suited to someone from a family of butchers. TFW made the occasional very fleeting appearance and it is on the extremely rare occasions when TFW visits the sick that you really do realise she is no more a vicar than Joe or Eddie Grundy.

She was of no help whatsoever for the most part, merely repeating, as if it were some kind of mantra, 'I'm a good listener', a phrase which would induce any self-respecting recipient to administer a knuckle sandwich. Surprisingly little was seen of Horrible Hayley and it appeared that her ostracism had been pretty thorough. She and Pat had a couple of 'glad we're still friends' sessions and then didn't speak to each other for months. Suddenly the psychiatric establishment's secret weapon was unleashed – just the person you want to see when you're on the edge – jolly old Mike Tugger. The counselling role fitted him like an ill-fitting glove and he made a few awkward visits to Pat, telling her, 'Oi've bin there. Oi know what you're goin' through.' Sensibly, Pat realised that the only way to avoid further visits was to get better. So off she went for a four-day visit to a nunnery in Wales, returning in a frame of mind to take on the sausage-producing world single-handed.

The first thing she did when she got back was to retract her comments about Tony being a murderer. This came as a huge disappointment to many, but we have to be stoical about these things. The greatest turnaround came when she offered to help Tommy with his sausages at the Farmers' Market. It then became obvious that the place she had visited in Wales that had brought about her recovery was not a religious establishment at all. In fact it was the equivalent of one of these courses for arachnophobes where they end up holding a spider. By the end of her four days of brainwashing, Pat was able to hold a sausage. It's just wonderful what can be done nowadays. As Pat's Welsh relations would no doubt tell us, 'Never say di.'

Treachery!
Mutiny in the Ambridge Cricket Team

Apart from boules and whingeing the most popular sport in Ambridge is cricket. Good old-fashioned cricket played on lazy summer afternoons and washed down by gallons of warm Shires. Like many village teams, Ambridge CC has had its ups and downs over the years. The frequent banishment of players to the realms of 'The Disappeared' does little to bolster the club's fortunes, but it has generally kept its head above water and occasionally enjoyed modest success.

At the helm have been a succession of captains motivated by a mixture of pride, bile and the inability to say *no* when asked to take on the job. The demise of one-time Captain Handbag Hebden caused the inception of the dreaded Single Wicket Competition, a contest that has brought almost as much grief and bitterness as 50lb of pork and leek sausages. But the darkest day in the club's history dawned at the end of the 1998 season.

The club captaincy had drifted into the hands of Sean Myerson. It was one of those classic situations where nobody would take on the role and then when a relative outsider agrees to do it, some of the more long-in-the-tooth club members mutter darkly about 'upstarts and interlopers'. The main objector was former club captain and homosceptic Sid Perks. His dislike of Sean was on two somewhat different grounds. His stated objection was that he 'batted the wrong way', a dreadfully un-PC notion in a village such as Ambridge, where coaches to Gay Pride rallies are regularly oversubscribed.

But Sid's main problem with Sean deserves considerably more sympathy than it is generally accorded. In essence, Sean moved the focal point of village cricket from the Bull to the Pink Cat. Warm beer is one thing but warm lager is quite another, and Sid was justifiably miffed when he lost a load of trade to another pub that was not even in the village. Anarchists have long suspected that the Cat is, in fact, a caravan, as it seems to have moved around a lot over the years, particularly in terms of its proximity to the village.

The 1998 season was not a good one for the Ambridge Cricket Club. They had frequent difficulties in mustering a team, which meant that the likes of Eddie Grundy were called up – always portentous of looming defeat. Results were appalling and the genial veneer of Sean gave way to snarling defensiveness.

The high points of the local cricket calendar are the games with Darrington which, over the years, have taken on the same intensity as an 'old firm' Rangers and Celtic match. Fat Man Forrest and Dan would turn up in days gone by, with Walter Gabriel in tow, all tooled up with broken bottles and Stanley knives. If you didn't end up with a good glassing, it was a pretty dull affair. Dirty tricks galore have been pulled over the years to try to get one over on the other side. Still fresh in the memory is a half-baked plan by Loopy Nigel and Dr Death to lure the best Darrington players away to non-existent county trials on the day of their match with Ambridge. But in 1998 it was all hopeless.

Sean's solution to the problem was to suggest a merger between Ambridge and Darrington, a suggestion so crass and insensitive as to defy belief. It was the kind of idea that could only come from an outsider with no sense of history. He convened secret talks and tried to enlist the support of the few decent Ambridge cricketers: Dayveed, Roy Tugger, Lancastrian Tommy and Dr Death.

The latter was a lost cause, as he was too busy making mincemeat of the Hippocratic oath. A general meeting was called to discuss the proposal and Shul-ugh was very much to the fore, invoking the name of Handbag and saying how he would have turned in his grave at the very idea. He would probably have turned somewhat more, reaching a creditable spin, at the idea of his wife making whoopee with the local doctor.

Ultimately loyalty won the day and there were just two Judases, in the form of young Tugger and Sean himself. Ambridge is an unforgiving village and Sean was punished for his treachery by having his voice box removed for several months. To add insult to injury Sean callously won the Single Wicket Trophy when he was meant to let Lancastrian Tommy have it as a consolation for having his brother squashed by a tractor.

Dayveed and Lancastrian Tommy deserve the highest praise for their loyalty. Having lost the captaincy of Sean, there was the usual unseemly wrangling and desperate search for a successor. Unsurprisingly the job went to Phallustair Blandvoice, one of the few speakers in the village who had not already held the uncoveted post.

There had been some question of bringing back Sid. With Sean now off the scene he seemed rather keen to return. He saw himself in the vein of some ousted Third World dictator returning to pick up the pieces. Instead he was given a spurious title of club manager on the strict understanding that it was to be completely meaningless. Initially he was happy enough with this but, of course, the main benefit to Sid was the fact that the focal point for village cricket was once more returned to the Bull. Presumably the Pink Cat had yet again got itchy feet and moved on up the road.

By the following season, the likes of Beddy Tugger had completely failed to realise the seriousness and truly treacherous nature of what had happened. She was heard cheerfully to say, 'You heard that Darrington beat Edgeley' as if half the village would suddenly don the Darrington colours in honour of her pig's bladder-toting son and the treacherous Mr Myerson.

It's not easy to make the Single Wicket Competition interesting. Once you've lost the trophy and all the characters have won it, what is there left to say? In 1999 there was the question of whether the traitors should be allowed to compete. The rules of the competition say that if you live in Ambridge you are allowed to enter the competition even if you have absconded to the enemy team. But you do have to live in Ambridge. This racist rule was introduced to discriminate against people from Penny Hassett, a nearby village in which all the residents are Somalis.

Roy Tugger, fearing a lynching, decided that discretion was the better part of cowardice and declined to take part. Sean Myerson also declined, but not until he'd wound up Sid to the point where he was pawing the ground. We were treated to some further discussion about Sean's proclivities and Sid's views when Right-on Kate suggested that one in ten of the male population is gay and therefore there must already be a gay member of the cricket team. Sid almost choked on his muesli at this concept.

It's certainly the case that Lancastrian Tommy has a rather

camp voice, but we don't actually know a full eleven members of the team so it's not too easy to 'out' someone. On the other hand, Darrington might have two gay members which could mean that Ambridge need not have any. Funny business, statistics.

The 1999 SWC was dull as ditchwater. The reserve trophy made a brief appearance while we went through the rather weary ritual of the current holder once more having such a huge house that they are able to lose a large tacky piece of mock-silverware. What we always have to remember is that Shul-ugh is unaware that there are two trophies, though why she should be concerned about this is open to question.

A new cricketer was born in the form of Elephant Man Christopher Carter. We all knew he was bowling when we heard the shrieks from the normally silent village children and the sound of mothers' aprons being desperately hidden behind. It was noticeably un-PC of someone to describe Christopher's bowling as 'unorthodox'. Most of us thought he had put his trunk to excellent use in bowling out Eddie Grundy.

Siobhan Hathaway, who is obviously in training as the village's latest sickly nice person, bowled out Tony. The ultimate in bathos was attained when Lancastrian Tommy picked up the award, although it was generally agreed among Anarchists that everyone else had thrown the game rather than have to put up with a repeat of the previous year's sulkathon. They didn't fancy having to go on permanent suicide watch at Bridge Farm – never the jolliest of places at the best of times.

One of the reasons that the team is so awful is that doctors and vets always play far too important a role, only to disappear at key moments to do unimportant things like tending sick people and animals. It was just such an occasion when Phallustair had been called away, presumably to murder a dog, that Sid stepped in to captain the team. His great tactical decision was to use nomark Neil Carter as a bowler on the basis that the opposition would be so surprised by the use of a non-bowler that their wickets would clatter. Sure enough, that is exactly what happened. And some people say the *Archers* aren't real. Bah.

Sid has found it exceptionally difficult to keep his ten-foot hooter out of playing matters, though we have to sympathise to some extent because super-wimp Phallustair is so obviously out of his depth. Indeed since Sid has taken on self-appointed duties as an intelligence gatherer, the team has shone.

The Cricket Club Dinner is usually a date worth putting in your diary. A few years ago, it was gatecrashed by the genial Mr Barraclough, devoted son of the late Mrs Barraclough, who accosted Dr Death in front of all his mates and accused him of murder. In 1999 Shul-ugh booked a Colonel Bridgwater as the guest speaker and he proceeded to spew forth a stream of offensive and risqué jokes. In a PC place like Ambridge, that must have been rather a hoot.

The long-term future of the cricket club should be fairly rosy, with the exploding birth rate in the village. And if you fancy placing a few bob down at Ladbrokes on a hot Anarchist tip, we reckon that it won't be too long before Roy Tugger comes crawling back to ACC with his tail between his stumpy legs.

The Role of Rogering
The Sexual History of Shul-ugh Hebden-Blandvoice

Known amongst Anarchists as Britain's most sexually active churchwarden, Shul-ugh Hebden-Blandvoice has never been reluctant to put it about. Newer listeners may only be aware of her penchant for the medical and veterinary professions, but the awful Shul-ugh has more notches on her bedpost than there are hassocks in St Stephen's. As far as we can determine the chronological order is as follows. Please bear in mind, however, that when you are dealing with numbers as huge as this, it is impossible to guarantee accuracy and we have had to rely on the human frailties of fading memories, together with one or two castist publications and hagiographies. We would also like to pay tribute to Anarchist Murray Craig, who wrote a learned treatise himself on this same subject and first alerted us to the full extent of St Shul-ugh's promiscuity. Indeed Mr Craig strongly asserted that 'Carolide', as Jeck Woolley adenoidally calls her, has wrongly been accorded the title of 'Village Bicycle'.

RICK Shul-ugh began as she meant to go on. This was her first recorded bloke, a married music freak in his thirties from

Borchester Tech (now known as University and famous for its useful honours degrees in Contemporary Lager Drinking and Lego Modelling). Although it is always said that this relationship began when she was fourteen, Anarchists strongly believe that she was really only eleven and it was typical of the BBC's tendency, even then, to sanctify Shul-ugh and gloss over her many indiscretions. Needless to say that Foghorn, although her voice was about two octaves higher in those days, was like a John Dory on heat while this relationship was going on.

WELSH BILL He was actually quite a nice guy, who had the advantage of having more than the shared brain cell employed by most of the characters in Ambridge. His cardinal error was that when he went for tea at Brookfield he failed to consume the statutory eight plates of Foghorn's scones and, more seriously, dared to discuss farming with Phil. It is sometimes the case that people do not realise that the Archer Mafia rule Ambridge and can do no wrong. Bill gave Phil the benefit of his opinions and even in those days the superficially saintly Shul-ugh would never do anything to jeopardise her inheritance.

ALL THE YOUNG CONSERVATIVES Remembering that this dates back to the days when Young Conservatives ruled the world, we are talking about serious numbers of blokes here. It would be invidious to single out any individual, although we know that loopy **NIGEL PARGETTER** was well in there, together with **TIM BEECHAM**. Tim was a member of the Borchester Branch of the Assassins, whose idea of a good night out was to drink yak's blood and brandy cocktails and throw up over the Lawson Hope memorial seat.

Another was **CHARLES HODGSON**. It was never quite clear why she didn't last longer with this bloke, because he was a well-loaded toff and very much a man of the horse. Perhaps his only crime was that he wasn't hung like one.

NEIL CARTER He was always sniffing around, and Shul-ugh may or may not have gone the distance with him as her bit of rough. She certainly led him on often enough.

HANDBAG HEBDEN She started knocking around with him a long time before their marriage and, in a style that she was to continue later on, she managed to indulge in some concurrence of bedfellows. For some years there would always be, as a standard character, a scribbler from the *Borchester Echo*. This tradition has ceased without explanation. **ROBIN CATCHPOLE** was one such person and breezed in and out of Shul-ugh's bed for a month or so. But he was only the warm-up act for a successor journalist, **SIMON PARKER**, who gave her a good old-fashioned seeing-to in a cornfield, upsetting a whole load of listeners who were so revolted that they couldn't face their suppers for several days.

Ludicrously, we were meant to believe that the cornfield incident was Shul-ugh's 'first time'. Perhaps the words 'that day' would put it into a more realistic context. Interestingly it was when Parker was offered a job outside of Ambridge that Shul-ugh refused to leave the village and the relationship ended – the same stunt she was to pull after seducing Dr Death many years later.

Some Spanish waiter called **PEDRO** and a complete **AUSTRALIAN SHEARING GANG** can be added to this immodest list, along with all the other male members of the Club 18–30 holiday groups or whatever travel companies she went with on her overseas holidays.

NICK WEARING The next in the queue, he was a bit of a lad, another rich farmer's son who worked his way around the available Ambridge womenfolk before pausing with Shul-ugh for a while. She went round the world with him except that he went round a bit more of the world than she did because he left her in Bangkok. Bearing in mind that Elizabeth was dumped by the great Cameron Fraser in a similarly remote and inhospitable location (the M1 services), it is coincidental but entirely understandable how these two sisters lend themselves to being abandoned.

BEN WARNER Another bit of rough for Shul-ugh was the burglar-cum-tramp Ben Warner with, whom she appeared to indulge in the occasional threesome, supplemented by Jackie Woodstock. This was also concurrent with her extremely lengthy engagement/courtship with Handbag Hebden. Throughout her marriage to Hebden she continually reverted to Loopy Nigel, whose charms are clearly well concealed over the radio. If it had not been that he was an SDP councillor with a mobile phone, one could have felt quite sorry for Mark.

HARD-WORKING SIMON PEMBERTON Pausing briefly to catch her breath when Hebden went to that great district council meeting in the sky, Shul-ugh's next port of call was Hard-working Simon Pemberton. All went smoothly enough and her bedsprings were duly put through their paces until she decided to play the pot to Simon's kettle. Just because he was giving some much-needed comfort to his former love, Mrs Harriet Williams, Shul-ugh went all huffy. Conveniently forgetting the string of blokes she had quadruple-timed, she became all churchwardenish and hit him.

PHALLUSTAIR BLANDVOICE She then went solo for the longest time in her history, until Phallustair Blandvoice arrived on the scene. Listeners will recall that the Village Bicycle immediately had her sights set on Phallustair, but it was all a bit complicated because he was more interested in Shul-ugh, whilst Graham Ryder was drooling over the Bicycle. To further complicate matters, Shul-ugh had gone into one of her temporary iron-knickered 'Oh, I've suddenly remembered I'm a churchwarden' modes and was not taking the Phallustair bait.

The fact that the Bicycle wanted Phallustair was sufficient to ensure that Shul-ugh would deny her best friend the opportunity, so there followed an extremely tedious period of Shul-ugh playing hard to get. But eventually she swore undying love for the drippy bloke and, within days of this, was seducing **DR DEATH** in an infamous and stomach-churning 'I want you now' scene.

With apologies to any more of the Ambridge males we might have omitted, we reckon that (seasonally adjusting the figures for the shearing gang, Young Conservatives and random holiday partners) Shul-ugh has managed to get through an average of two or three men per year since she has been fourteen.

Careful study of the types of men she has ensnared over the years will indicate a gradual change from the initial alternation between farm hands and wealthy farmers' sons to the present day when she insists on professional qualifications and a healthy bank balance.

Quiz Two
A Who's Who for the Seasoned Listener

These questions are pretty difficult on the assumption that most normal people do not retain sufficient trivia to remember all kinds of characters who haven't shown up for years. If you manage to answer more than half of them, you should take a serious look at yourself, because you're probably the sort of person who always has a large space round them at parties. You're generally at your happiest in the 'Five items or less queue' at the supermarket counting how many items other customers have in their baskets.

Questions

1. What was the name of the woman from the pony club with whom Brian went the distance?
2. What were the names of the two boys fostered by Tom and Pru?
3. What is the name of Boring George Barford's previous wife?
4. What is the name of his daughter?
5. Who is Rosemary Tarrant?
6. What is the name of Carol Tregorran's daughter?
7. Who left a small legacy to Neil to enable him to carry on his minor farming enterprises?
8. Who was Fairlie?
9. Nora McCauley, as she had reverted to calling herself by the time she left the village, married someone else prior to shacking up with Boring George. Who?
10. Who was the fierce cleaning woman who terrorised Mrs High and Mighty Aldridge?

Answers

1. Mandy Beesborough.
2. Peter Stevens and Johnny Martin.
3. Ellen.
4. Karen.
5. Nelson Gabriel's daughter.
6. Anne.
7. Bill Insley (extra point for noting that he was one of the most boring people ever to darken the airwaves).
8. Laura's housekeeper.
9. Greg Salt.
10. Mrs Walker.

Something of the Night
The Sinister World of Damien Hebden

Shul-ugh's son, Damien, was the result of numerous experiments in genetic engineering. Anarchists never lavish much pity on Shul-ugh, but her endless attempts with Handbag Hebden to conceive naturally before giving birth to a Dalek did at least demonstrate a degree of tenacity. He is living, if a little extraterrestrial, proof of the dangers of GM trials.

In a desperate attempt to exorcise the obvious demonic characteristics of the little brat, Shul-ugh went through the motions of giving him a christening. It has to be said that none of the church services at St Stephen's is what we would regard as 'normal', and the guests at the christening all turned up with cloves of garlic and iron stakes, so essential in his presence. The idea of calling him Daniel should be recognised for what it was, a rather over-used PR stunt in Ambridge whereby you give a child a name in honour of the most financially loaded relation. It is meant to be a good investment for the future.

Thus the late Jaaaarn was christened John Daniel in the hope that some of ancient Dan's wonga might percolate through to the impoverished crowd at Bridge Farm. Needless to say, when Dan was fatally savaged by a sheep, Jaaaarn inherited diddly squat – not that it would have made any difference as it turned out. Damien was christened Daniel because the avaricious Shul-ugh, already having copped Glebe Cottage when she murdered Doris, was determined to butter up her parents in order to stay in the frame for a bit of Brookfield in due course. It was a similar motivation that led to Peeeep being named after Phil.

Damien has never really had a decent chance in life. His mother is a confirmed nymphomaniac; indeed, not only is she confirmed but she's a churchwarden as well. Damien must have become confused by the endless procession of men trooping through the house. As Joe Grundy so brilliantly encapsulated the situation, 'First the doctor, then the vet – it's a good job there isn't a dentist in Ambridge.'

Early signs of Damien's demonic nature appeared when he alternated baby gurgling with lucid, properly structured sentences, apparently being able to switch between them at will. He gradually abandoned the gurgling, but maniacally insisted on answering all questions with full sentences. 'Do you like going to feed the ducks, Daniel?' would be answered not by a simple 'Yes' or a decent grunt, but by, 'Yes, I do'.

Mountaineering Teddy, a gift from the much-missed Hardworking Simon Pemberton, seemed to play a formative role in Damien's development. Since Shul-ugh has long since ceased to refer to it, we can only assume that she incinerated it in a pagan ritual before Damien's very eyes, no doubt adding to his torment.

Another factor which will have done much to distort Damien's outlook on life is Phallustair's propensity to lie to him. Phallustair is one of those people who delights in confusing children by building up a huge world of non-existent people, such as Father Christmas, the Tooth Fairy *et al*. Filling the little brat's head with stories of animals that speak and magic is enough to send even a normal child completely over the edge. Perhaps the final straw came when Phallustair claimed that a certificate in a frame on a wall was about to sound a trumpet fanfare – a notion so ludicrous that it should have sounded alarm bells throughout the village.

In a weird reversal of normality Damien has increasingly sought the comfort of his mother's bed as he has got older. We have the grotesque prospect in years to come of nineteen-year-old Damien banishing Phallustair from the bedroom on the grounds that the bed is too small for three. In fact, maybe we should be referring to him from now on as Oedipus.

Damien is noticeably restless and ill at ease when he has to accompany his sanctimonious mother on one of her numerous trips to church. The presence of so many crosses clearly does his head in. When he had to attend the Palm Sunday service and TFW was actually handing out palm crosses to all comers, he was beside himself and tried desperately to concentrate on the more secular side of the proceedings. His principal interest was the thorny question of whether the donkey would or would not 'do a pooh'. (See 'That Fisher Woman: The Case Against'.)

As time goes on, listeners must be prepared for intermittent manifestations of the forces of darkness. Incidents will occur which at first sight may appear unfortunate accidents, but as they mount up it will become apparent that the hand of the Devil is well and truly at work.

An example of this has already arisen – the knee-capping of Foghorn, an early and amazing triumph for Damien. In the light of the plummeting standards of *Archers* language, it was what one might uncouthly describe as 'a piece of piss'. All he had to do was to deposit a toy car on the stairs at Brookfield. Foghorn was in full flight, rushing downstairs with bedding for her B&B guests, and Bob's yer uncle. Nice one. Foghorn was naturally completely blind to the fact that Damien was to blame and instead said it was all the fault of the guests for whom she was fetching the bedding. We live in a strange world in which B&B guests should sleep without bedding and toy cars are regarded as a legitimate form of stair-carpeting.

Damien revelled in his grandmother's discomfort and was later described as having got 'carried away playing with Jill's crutches'. Numerous comments from other characters give testimony to his true nature, including: 'Inside every little angel there's a devil trying to get out' and 'He's a little monster.' So you don't just have to take our word for it.

We have heard how Damien will insist that the dreadful Shul-ugh plays his favourite tape of 'children's songs' on car journeys. But what she and Phallustair are too dense to realise is that if you play the tape backwards you can hear concealed messages – 'I'm going to trip my Granny', 'The Devil is king', 'Jamie Perks is next' being just some of them.

Whereas most well-adjusted four-year-olds have nice normal toys like sub-machine-guns, air rifles and Swiss Army knives to play with, Damien has an inflatable crocodile. This is doubtless to get him used to the genre so that he can have the real thing to terrorise the neighbourhood with by the time he is five. That would not be altogether bad news, as a crocodile in the Am would do wonders to spice up the tedious raft races.

Foghorn may be smugly limping around congratulating herself on surviving the assassination attempt, but there are two other members of Damien's family who have a fatwah out on them. BSE Josh and his stepfather Dayveed conspired to dispose of Damien's 'Muzzi'. After Josh had ceremoniously dragged it through the farmyard, Dayveed calmly incinerated it with the same cool detachment with which he killed the badger and murdered Jethro. But few would want to be in those people's shoes with Damien just waiting for his moment.

Damien's cousin Peeeep is a similarly sinister little girl who appears to be consumed by hatred for all around her. She had lain dormant for a couple of years since commenting on one of her school colleagues, saying, 'There's Stephen, I don't like Stephen', but was moved to squeak once more when urged by her mother, Roooooth, to play with Damien. 'I don't want to. I'm fed up with Daniel,' she quoth, presumably because she had tired of playing the much loved children's game of Vampires and Victims. But it is yet another indication that Damien is a malevolent force. Out of the mouths of babes ...

These You Have Loathed

In order to become members of the Archers Anarchist Experience it is necessary not only to bite off the head of a chicken but also to bare your soul to reveal your *Archers*-related preferences. This gives us invaluable data that we are now able to share exclusively with the wider public. We are constantly assailed by commercial organisations (usually manufacturers of anoraks and supermarket meals-for-one) seeking access to our mailing lists. It is important to state that under no circumstances would we consider acceding to such requests.

Naturally the most loved or hated characters are something of a movable feast according to their antics at the time. The following list is the Top Ten most hated characters as nominated by the most recent people to join our ranks. Independently analysed and authenticated as a scientific sample by a top pollster, it makes stunning reading:

Note to boffins – the percentages are calculated after excluding from the sample votes for those characters who did not reach the Top Ten.

1.	Shul-ugh	37%
2.	Rooooooth	17%
3.	Peggoi	10%
4.	Damien	10%
5.	Jailbird Carter	6%
6.	Phallustair	5%
7.	Foghorn	4%
8	TFW	4%
9	Usha	4%
10.	Kathy	3%

One or two misguided critics of our movement will look at this list and see its near total domination by Ambridge's womenfolk as evidence of misogyny on our part. It may therefore be helpful to point out that 60 per cent of our members are themselves women and this list reflects the views of our mass membership. It is also worth noting that this list was compiled prior to the arrival of the ludicrous Solly the Wally Pritchard or Slippery Simon Gerrard. They would unquestionably reach the Top Ten.

Shul-ugh has a clear and unassailable lead and if you add in the respectable percentages for Phallustair and Damien, the occupants of Glebe Cottage currently attract more than half the vote – no mean feat in a village of such obnoxious people.

These You Have Loved
(And Ignored)

Extensive statistical research has found it much more difficult to identify a strong list of characters in terms of popularity. Again, for the benefit of boffins we should point out that we calculated percentages after excluding those characters beyond the Top Ten. But, in contrast to the list of loathed characters, there were numerous people whose positive rating came very close to those in the Top Ten. This indicates that listeners are far more divided about whom they love than whom they hate. Twas not always so. When Archers Anarchists was founded in 1995, Nelson Gabriel – the man who put the cottage into honeysuckle – topped the popularity poll by a giddy mile and it is only his unexplained disappearance to the Bolivian rain forests that has removed him from our esteem. Even now, a staggering 44 per cent of Anarchists nominated him as the character they would most like to see return.

1.	Lynda	17%
2.	Brian	17%
3.	Horrible Hayley	12%
4.	Fat Clarrie	12%
5.	Eddie	11%
6.	Joe	8%
7.	The Village Bicycle	6%
8.	Loopy Nigel	6%
9	Marjorie	6%
10.	Joan Pargetter	5%

Given the large number of characters nominated as favourite (38) or most hated (30), another fascinatingly riveting fact is the number of current characters whom nobody chose at all. The role of the ignored included PHIL, NEIL, SEAN, MIKE, BEDDY and ROY TUGGER, and TONY. It must be quite galling for some of the mainstays of the village that no one gives a toss about them, and for the Tuggers to be ignored *en masse* is the epitome of humiliation.

'Do You Mind If I Stand?'
The Perils of Sitting Down in Ambridge

Anyone who is the wrong side of eighty would do well to stay on their pins in Ambridge. Anarchist investigations have revealed a disturbing number of incidences of 'death by sitting'. In the rest of the world people die of *something*, but in Ambridge they die 'peacefully in their chair'. Doris Archer, Fat Man Forrest and his wife, Pru, Martha Woodford, Mabel Larkin and, we presume, her husband, Ned, all seemed to meet their end in a sedentary position. The first thing elderly people in Ambridge should do is to get rid of their armchairs and sofas. It could make a real difference to their life expectancy.

Of course, the truth is that innocent furniture is being made a scapegoat for murder. For example, spot the connection in these two facts: Shul-ugh found Doris dead in her armchair; Shul-ugh inherited Glebe Cottage.

The deaths of Fat Man and Pru were even more sinister. It would be usual to hold some kind of inquest when a husband and wife popped their clogs within days of each other in the same old folks' home, but in Ambridge this coincidence went quite unnoticed. Instead it was seized upon as a good opportunity for another pagan funeral with Horrible Hayley, the Angel of Death, more or less officiating. The motive for murder was revealed soon after this double death when Phil triumphantly presented Foghorn with Pru's recipe books, with the words, 'You knew she was going to leave them to you, didn't you?' There can be no doubt that Phil and Foghorn had ample motive, as serial cooks, to remove Fat Man and Pru from the scene. But it was most unfair that a couple of blameless armchairs should once again carry the can.

Poor Martha Woodford actually died from the neglect of her so-called friends and neighbours. No one had mentioned her for months until suddenly she was found quietly dead at home, doubtless in a chair. Perhaps it would be helpful if MFI, IKEA and the rest could invent a symbol to designate the safety of its furniture in terms of general mortality rather than mere fire resistance – a tasteful skull and crossbones would do the trick.

Mrs Perkins, Peggoi's mother, was described in the *BOA* as being found by Mrs High and Mighty Aldridge 'sitting peacefully in her chair'. This was just another example of an Archer conveniently being at the scene of death. And we shouldn't be misled by all this 'peacefully' stuff. When you are dead in your chair you are hardly likely to be doing the Lambada, are you?

Bill Insley was similarly found at home in his chair although, as with Doris, there was another pair of worrying facts to bear in mind. Bill was 'found' by Neil. Neil was a beneficiary of his will. Perhaps this is why Neil, though in many ways a complete divot, seems sufficiently tuned in to the inherent dangers of a sedentary life in Ambridge, because he was recently heard to say, 'I've spent more time in a tractor cab than I have in my own armchair'. (See also 'Tractor Work'). And if he knows what's good for him, he'll keep it that way.

Quiz Three
At Home in Ambridge: The Criminal World

These questions all relate to the general lawlessness of Archers characters over the years. They serve as a sober reminder of just what kind of a place Ambridge and its environs really is.

Questions

1. Shul-ugh, despite her sanctimonious nature, is of course a convicted criminal. Of what offence was she convicted?
2. Which former boyfriend of Shul-ugh's was imprisoned for burglary?
3. What problem did Sid's criminal past give him later on when he wanted to go straight?
4. Why did Jailbird Carter lose remission?
5. What was the name of the man for whom Sid worked at the time of the Mailbag Robbery who was actually involved in that crime?
6. What was Terry Barford's first known crime?
7. Of what crime was Neil convicted?
8. Who was wrongly acquitted for murder?
9. Who murdered Jethro Larkin and with what weapon?
10. Who poisoned Patch using illegal bait?

Answers

1. Taking and driving away.
2. Ben Warner.
3. He was not able to be a licensee.
4. Because she went off to Hebden's funeral.
5. Mr Brown.
6. Breaking and entering.
7. Possession of drugs.
8. Fat Man Forrest.
9. Dayveed, with a tree branch.
10. George Boring-Barford.

Castism
How to Avoid It

It was the need to challenge castism that brought Archers Anarchists into being. Listeners will doubtless agree that the radio is a far superior form of medium to the goggle-box, whose presence aggressively dominates the living rooms of the majority of our population. It enables us to sharpen our listening faculties and powers of imagination, an activity that television denies us.

Castism is a cruel betrayal of all the efforts we have made to respond to and embrace the wonders of radio. It cocks a snook at the loyalty we have shown as *Archers* listeners. We willingly indulged the late Dan Archer, Patriarch of Ambridge, in his need for four radically different voices throughout his lifetime. No one was discourteous enough to suggest that this was anything other than an endearing idiosyncrasy. But, in return, the BBC, demonstrating crass insensitivity, permitted the publication of four equally different photographs of 'Dan'. Not even the greatest master of disguise could seek to pass off four people of different build, height, skin texture etc. as the same person. So what on earth were we meant to think? The fact is that we didn't need to see photos of Dan because *we* had already decided what he looked like.

Over the years, things have gone from bad to worse as castism has increased. The tendency for characters from *The Archers* to make 'public appearances' at shows, fêtes and other functions is quite deplorable. What is particularly upsetting is that it can be difficult to avoid encountering these imitators. The argument 'You don't have to look at them' is of no relevance if you are ambling around some country show only to find yourself suddenly face to face with a hat with horns. Similarly, if you are standing in a queue for a cup of tea and the person in front of you starts chatting away at 190 decibels, you may unwittingly have invaded the airspace of Foghorn.

Unfortunately, castism is not confined to offensive photographs and characters exposing themselves in public. A more subtle form is the tendency of people to talk about 'actors'.

The formation of the 'official' fan club of *The Archers*, a BBC-controlled Mafia known to its many enemies as Archers Anoraks, has done much to encourage the growth of castism and the perpetration of castist remarks. The Anoraks produce huge quantities of tacky merchandise, much of it inevitably bearing attempted photographic representation of things which should by rights be confined to the mind.

It is difficult to understand what kind of warped mentality can lead someone to listen to *The Archers* and then cough up £1,500 to go on a cruise with a bunch of luvvies claiming to be 'characters'. Any genuine listener will know that very few people in Ambridge ever go on holiday, and the idea of any of them going off on a cruise together is risible. Yet these castist cruises are regular events. Has anyone ever heard someone in Ambridge say, 'I'm off for a couple of weeks on a freebie cruise with a load of Anoraks'?

A particularly unpleasant manifestation of castism from the

dreaded Anoraks is called 'The Ambridge Experience'. It consists of a weekend in some Fat Cat country house hosted by Foghorn. The idea of paying vast sums to be deafened for two days seems quite perverse.

Archers Anoraks are regularly advertised at the taxpayers' expense on Radio 4. Archers Anarchists can lay claim to some slight influence in that the BBC now invariably describes the Anoraks as 'the only official fan club'. This is a strange phenomenon afflicting many institutions that attract fan clubs, namely the tendency to label themselves 'official'. It is difficult to conceive of any benefit that can be derived from being 'official', save for the fact that you will probably be charged more and restricted in your freedom to criticise or comment upon the institution concerned.

Ideally, Borsetshire characters should remain in that walled county. But sadly this is difficult to enforce, so we have to give you a few handy tips on avoiding castist situations. No one can be completely safe from castism, but if you follow the simple precautions outlined in our Ten Point Plan below, you will greatly reduce your chances of becoming a victim.

1. Avoid agricultural shows (gratuitous appearances by numerous 'characters'). This has the added benefit of allowing you to miss out on people with green wellies, four-wheel drives and straw hanging out of their mouths loudly blaming whichever government happens to be in power for the fact that they have to get up early and milk cows.

2. Never buy Country and Western records/CDs. Eddie Grundy has a nasty habit of releasing them from time to time and putting his face on the sleeves.

3. Beware of any archive material from the late 'Eddie Grundy Fan Club'. Worthy though it was, Eddie was prone to appear in person at its functions, and alleged pictorial representation would follow in their newsletters.

4. Do not go to see any enticingly worded events at art centres, e.g. 'An evening with *The Archers*'. Remember that the only genuine evening with *The Archers* occurs nightly, except Saturdays, at 7.02 p.m.

5. Avoid paying four-figure sums of money to go in big boats. If you really want to see a load of water, just leave the bath running.

6. Never buy the *Radio Times*. They take a delight in publishing random castist photographs without warning. They also publish an offensive item called a 'cast list'.

7. Never buy a broad-sheet newspaper when there has been a 'big' story in *The Archers*. With true contempt for their readers' capacity for simple comprehension, they take the view that it is impossible to write a story about a radio programme without illustrating it with a photograph.

8. If you ever buy or receive any *Archers*-related book, other than those bearing the Archers Anarchist seal of approval, be aware that it is virtually unknown for any of these to be free of castism – both photographic and verbal. If you feel it is absolutely necessary to have the book, ensure that someone removes the photographs beforehand. Even then, you are liable to find heavily castist content within the text.

9. If you suddenly hear a monotonous Geordie whingeing sound, run for your life – Roooooth's loose.

10. If someone says to you something along the lines of 'Did you know the actor who plays **** has died?', try a subtle form of put-down such as, 'And what actor plays you, sad git?'

Educated Ambridge
The Ofsted Report

In these days of constant talk about class sizes and league tables it is something of a national scandal that nothing has been done to address the appalling level of education in the village of Ambridge and presumably its surrounding area. Sadly the priorities there seem to be 'Fornication, fornication and fornication'. We can only assume that Ofsted have refused to go into Borchester because they don't want to admit the complete failure of the teaching profession to produce a properly educated pupil from the town or its environs over the last twenty to thirty years.

Not that people haven't occasionally gone on to further education. One or two high-flyers have tried in vain to complete the odd vocational course in Applied Stamp Licking or Comic Reading. So, once again, it falls to Anarchists to expose the educational performance of Ambridge's children.

We thought the best way of producing a report was to look at the educational histories of a number of characters through the years from a range of families in order to demonstrate that we are not talking merely of a flash in the imbecilic pan. What we will seek to show is that, regardless of family background or the cost of their education, Ambridge children are as thick as two short planks.

ADAM MACY is the exception that proves the rule. He allegedly graduated from Newcastle University but, as he has never been seen or heard since, we take this with a pinch of Brian's genetically modified crops. If he genuinely did get through university it is nothing short of a miracle, because his schooling was a complete joke. Partly because he'd had rather an excess of dads, thanks to his mother's sexual peccadilloes, he was refusing to work at school and Brian poured large wads of his hard-earned cash into third-rate fee-paying schools. His total disappearance is extremely sinister.

DAYVEED ARCHER was the classic Archer dumb cluck. He went to a boarding school despite his mother's socialist principles, and what a waste of wonga that turned out to be. He failed his maths A-level repeatedly, which goes a long way to explaining the parlous state of the finances at Brookfield in recent years. University was about as likely as Kathy Perks doing a stint behind the bar in the Bull, so instead he followed in the footsteps of a number of the educationally if not financially challenged and went to agricultural college.

DEBBIE ALDRIDGE actually went to Exeter University, but before anyone gets over-excited at this exceptional example of scholarliness, it has to be pointed out that she only lasted a year. She succumbed to an acute attack of what might nowadays be referred to as Woodheaditis. It all came about because she was studying the extremely useful subject of French Canadian Literature, a course which was later to stand her in such good stead in the lambing shed.

It is also written in the tea leaves that if there is an unsuitable bloke within a radius of 100 miles, Debbie will become magnetically drawn to him. Such was the case with her lecturer in the aforementioned subject, Simon Gerrard, who has, of course, made a long overdue reappearance. She rapidly got herself into a Pembertonesque situation with him of the 'Yes, please, I mean no thanks, how dare you' variety. To be fair to her, with a pedigree of one failed year at university behind her, Debbie is still a contender for Brain of Borsetshire.

ELIZABETH PARGETTER, whose brains have always proved elusiv, failed her Eleven-Plus, which, in the state sector, would have condemned her to an early teenage life among the great unwashed. Happily, Red Foghorn rode to the rescue with another minor private boarding school. She was expelled from that school, an honour not even bestowed on the Grundys.

Without any qualifications she went to the penitentiary for all the Ambridge thickoes formerly known as Borchester Tech, now laughingly renamed 'University'. But Elizabeth even manage to fail at the tech, a feat never previously achieved, even by Ambridge youngsters. The stresses and strains of studying Contemporary Sandcastle Studies had proved too much. She never really ventured back into the world of academia and has not since acquired any skills in anything other than mother-in-law baiting.

The mystery of why anyone would want her to present courses in marketing a couple of years ago was soon solved when it was revealed that these courses involved a mattress and a bloke called Horny Hugh. Perhaps we are being slightly unfair to Elizabeth, as she has at least become a practitioner of the world's oldest profession.

THE LATE JAAAARN ARCHER Jaarn was a canny self-made sort of chap from an entrepreneurial perspective, but as far as academic achievement was concerned there was no evidence that he was any better than the rest of the village. He was another of the victims of at least a partial private education and was sent to a place called Brymore – a name that is more redolent of a young offenders' institution than a seat of learning. There was never any serious question of a university education, although being squashed by a tractor rather limited his future educational options.

KATE ALDRIDGE eschewed every educational opportunity and failed to achieve even the most rudimentary qualifications. She started off at the posh Cheltenham Ladies' College, where she just ran amok, and was transferred to the local sink school, Borchester Green, that houses all the low-life such as the Grundys, Horrobins, Tuggers and Carters.

So appalling were Kate's results that the educational psychos even got involved and we had an amusing period when the Aldridges were dragged into 'family therapy'. Brian diagnosed that this was a load of sociological nonsense and gave it a wide berth. After a great deal of pointless hoo-ha Kate went to Borchester Tech, the repository for recidivist non-achievers. All she succeeded in doing there was to make friends with some of Borchester's finest, such as Messrs Spanner and Craven – purveyors of fine excrement.

KENTON ARCHER There is a very misleading line in the *BOA* which describes Kenton as a 'star pupil' at Borchester Grammar. The words which should have been added were *relatively speaking*. It is quite obvious that, within a catchment area of the most obtuse children ever to walk on Bishop Cyril's earth, it is not difficult to star. It presumably entails being able to write your name, maybe tie your shoelaces and find your way home with the aid of a school bus. That he failed to go on to university but instead went into the 'merchant' navy says it all.

LANCASTRIAN TOMMY The first we knew about Tommy's education was when he came of voice, albeit a Lancastrian one, and threw both a huge party and up in the village hall to celebrate the completion of his GCSEs. And there his education ended. He embarked upon some NVQ course in farming. For those who are not up to date on modern pre-/post-millennium qualifications it should be explained that an NVQ isn't one. So Tommy has basically signed up for an NVQ in moping around the farm with an attitude problem, which he looks like achieving with room to spare.

LUCY PERKS Girls in Ambridge perform slightly better academically than boys – a rare example in *The Archers* of life imitating life – and Lucy appeared against all the odds of a broken and fractious home to get through Nottingham University and emerge with a degree. True it was in Environmental Science and so presumably concentrated on how to build a tree-house or tunnel near a proposed motorway site. But, in the eyes of the Lord, a degree is a degree and in the village of Ambridge it is as rare a sight as a barking dog on one of their farms. Note again that as with Adam she has completely disappeared since 'graduating'.

SHUL-UGH HEBDEN-BLANDVOICE is another educational disaster. According to the aforementioned *BOA*, Shul-ugh was actually regarded as 'backward' at her primary school. This could explain a lot – whether they were talking about her intellect or favourite posture. She went to Borchester

Grammar, but as per usual there is no evidence of her getting any qualifications of note because she went on to that scholastic graveyard 'Borchester Tech' to do a secretarial course.

She took a number of examinations at Rodway and Watson, which seemed to involve numerous failures and retakes, and her very gradual promotion doubtless owed more to sexual favours granted to Mr Rodway than to any endeavours on her part. When she was ceremoniously booted out of the firm for gross misconduct there was never any mention of her having any estate management qualifications that she could tout round to other companies. More recently she has once more donned a dunce's cap, this time in the form of a horse rider's hard hat, as she has struggled with horse-riding exams. It really has been painful to behold.

ROY TUGGER Poor Roy has manfully tried to crawl out from the abyss that is life as a Tugger. The *BOA* actually tells a downright lie, describing him as 'bright'. Let there be no mistake here, Roy is about as bright as a 20-watt bulb. We have to remember that this is a bloke who was prepared to go to court to prove that he was the father of a Caribbean baby. His education has been a paradigm of Ambridge learning, culminating in about one and a half GCSEs and a painful course of study at what he cringingly describes as 'Uni', from where he will emerge, to his parents' eternal pride, with a BA Hons in Gum Chewing.

SHARON RICHARDS It is one of the great unfairnesses of Ambridge life that Sharon was effectively banished from the village following the death of her beloved Jaaaarn. Anyone would think that it was she, not Horrible Hayley, who had callously turned down his proposal of marriage, thus inducing him to put the Fergie on autopilot. But we digress. Sharon was not allowed to emerge from school with any qualifications lest she show up the comparative ignorance of the Archer Mafia. So the peak of educational excellence so far as Sharon was concerned was a YTS placement with a hairdresser.

Herein lies yet another *Archers* mystery, for Sharon dropped out of this taxing form of quasi-employment as soon as she was swept off her feet and on to her back by the debonair Clive Horrobin. Anyone with experience of the hairdressing profession will know that the junior employees do not get anywhere near a pair of scissors. Their role is confined to making tea, washing customers' hair and asking them if they are going on holiday (or, during the period 1 August to 24 December, what they are doing for Christmas), in readiness for the stylist who will repeat the question moments later.

A YTS placement with a hairdresser would, of course, be somewhat below the rank just described. This role would include going out to buy the tea, sweeping up hair and rifling through corporation rubbish tips in the hope of unearthing the odd five-year-old copy of *She* magazine for the delectation of waiting customers.

The mystery is that Sharon was always deemed to be an excellent hairdresser and a whole variety of the Ambridge women would regularly beg her to cut their hair. She must therefore have been possessed of a wonderful innate talent requiring no training at all. We live in hope that she will return to the village one day as the owner of a string of successful salons. But the fact remains she was no academic.

WIWYERM GRUNDY No one would expect Wiwyerm to be the local chairman of MENSA and his educational performance has been generally predictable. Grange Farm is the kind of place where, in a more normal village, the Social Services would have their own parking space, such would be the frequency of their visits.

Wiwyerm has been a professional truant for some years. The most remarkable thing in recent times is that while he seemed to miss about four days' schooling in every five, he never came up with any explanation other than 'study days' or 'teacher training days'. Yet half the people to whom he trotted out these falsehoods gave him the benefit of the doubt. The *BOA* says that he went to Loxley Barrett Primary School. Both that school and the village itself are mentioned with comparative rarity. Indeed the fact that Wiwyerm apparently hated the school so much can, no doubt, be put down to the fact that he was its only pupil.

Wiwyerm seemed set to escape school unencumbered by any GCSEs, but an unholy alliance of the completely uneducated George Barford and Jeck Woolley conspired to entice him to do a masters degree in Keepering. How academic study can equip you for a life wandering around woodland in wellington boots and a wax jacket, carrying a gun, is open to question. But, all in all, this gentleman very much matches the scholastic standards of the village.

In recent times the unlikely named couple Bunty and Reg, parents of the late Handbag Hebden, have shown an interest in the education of the dreadful Damien. Seemingly unaware of his demonic nature, they wanted him to go to a local church school. The likely consequence of sending him to St Beelzebub's and All Vampires is unimaginable, but Phallustair came out as violently anti private school.

Though it has never prevented Foghorn from sending her children to boarding schools and grammar schools, she is also totally opposed to such things. Old footage of *The Archers* from when her voice was a veritable high-pitched scream and more like a police siren than a foghorn has her remonstrating with Phil over plans to send their children to Borchester Grammar.

For the sake of other children, Damien should, of course, be educated by a governess. But Phallustair for once seemed to exert influence over Shul-ugh, because she decided to send the brat to the local sink school at Loxley, thus setting the seal on a guaranteed career for her son as a demonic dunderhead.

The attitude of people in the village to education is generally very negative. Tony Archer was quoted as saying, 'Exams never did me any good', while the likes of Boring George Barford and Eddie Grundy have more or less colluded in allowing Wiwyerm to bunk off school. Poor Clarrie has done her best to maintain educational standards in the household, but it is rather pathetic listening to her giving help with revision: 'What's the past tense of Avwaar?'

Ultimately and ironically, this whole discussion is itself academic. If you are going to pursue a career in tractor work, poaching, whingeing or murder – a list that accounts for most of the Ambridge population – education just doesn't matter.

Anna Kissed
Answers Your Problems

Being an *Archers* listener can be psychologically challenging. Mindful of this, Archers Anarchists has retained a highly trained counsellor, caring Anna Kissed, to answer some of your *Archers*-related problems. Here is a selection of the more titillating ones.

Dear Anna,
I've always considered myself a fairly typical mother of eight who wouldn't generally hurt a fly (well, apart from discharging the odd burst of Vapona in its direction, that is). But I find that when I hear the sanctimonious tones of that Shul-ugh Hebden-Blandvoice I lose all sense of reason. Before I know where I am, I'm frothing at the mouth and wishing all kinds of disaster upon her and that possessed creature Damien. I also want to set fire to Mountaineering Teddy, until all that's left of him is the dangerous bits that the Hong Kong manufacturers used for his eyes and nose, which I then want Damien to be made to eat. What can I do to calm myself down?
The Rev Trixie Horrobin
Edgeley

Anna says:
I get many letters about this problem and I think you have to look at the cause – Shul-ugh. Now she's back involved with horse-riding again, you might try slotting a small wasps' nest under her saddle before she takes a summer ride. That should do the trick.

Dear Anna,
I am the under-manageress in a country house hotel, a job I've held now for some years. My problem is that I'm not allowed to speak. Whilst I find this no problem at night, I do think I could be a more effective manager if I was allowed to talk to staff and customers occasionally. Matters are not helped by having a receptionist who thinks she's the owner and I'm clearly in no position to disagree. Any suggestions?
T. Porter
Flatchester

Anna says:
Have you tried openly defying the ban? I can think of a number of precedents for this – Lancastrian Tommy, Sloane Helen, Loopy Nigel, Roy Tugger, to name but a few. All these people suddenly chirped up after years of silence and no one said, 'I've never heard you speak before' or 'Shut up!' I think you'd be surprised how receptive people would be. And if you don't like the sound of your voice, you can then go quiet again for a few years and have another go with a completely different voice a bit later.

Dear Anna,

Although it is over a year since 'Misery Monday' when the BBC shortened each episode of 'The Archers' AND made them start at approximately 7.03 p.m., I still find myself tuning in at 7.00 p.m., thus wasting three minutes per day. I am growing increasingly worried about the effect this may be having on my life. Can you help?

Concerned Listener

Name and address supplied

Anna says:

The short answer to your question is, of course, no. You are wasting valuable time each day when you could be boiling an egg. And if it makes you feel any worse, you might reflect that, assuming this affliction also ails you on a Sunday, you are wasting more than fifteen and a half hours a year – more or less the equivalent of a day.

Dear Anna,

A while back I made some chilli jam using one of the late Pru Forrest's favourite recipes. It was one that she had got off the even later Mrs Turvey. Sadly it took the roof of my mouth off and I've never been able to speak since. Do I have any redress in law?

Jean Harvey

Bull Farm, Ambridge

Anna says:

You might try going to Dr Wonderman Hathaway. The sun appears to shine out of his every orifice and you will doubtless find that with his army training such things as replacing the odd mouth roof are meat and drink to him.

Dear Anna,

I recently had a faintly disconcerting experience in the Bull whilst eating one of the dainty pieces of quasi-excrement that passes for a bar snack. On this occasion Freda Fry had rustled up a lightly microwaved pasty. It was well down to its usual rock-bottom standard when I discovered a horse's hoof in the filling. It occurred to me that it might be part of the late and largely forgotten Ippy. I didn't like to make a fuss because you know how Kathy hates customers. Also, due to my social class, speaking was of course out of the question, but I did feel afterwards that I should have alerted someone. What should I do?

Silent Person

The Council Houses, Ambridge

Anna says:

I'm not sure I understand the problem.

The Winter Cuckoo
Things That Only Happen in Ambridge

One of the many joyous facets of Archers Anarchists is the network of unfortunate people who notice every little wrinkle in our glorious programme. They are vigilant to the last in spotting those peculiarities in Ambridge life that set the villagers apart from the rest of us. The equivalent idiosyncrasies in television can apparently be found in *Coronation Street*, where someone orders a pint of beer, begins drinking it and is then clearly seen to have more in the glass three seconds later than he had moments before. But on radio pointed ears of the highest specifications are needed to do a proper monitoring job.

Cheep Cheep

While many of us just regard birds as things that tweet in a rather pointless and random way, Anarchist Chris Webster has dedicated his life to the recognition of Ambridge birdsong. He suggests that anachronistic tweeting is endemic in the village, but his most dramatic observation to date was the presence of cuckoos in September. Ambridge has always had problems with this particular bird. There have been years when it has been deemed compulsory to impose a 90-decibel cuckoo throughout the conventional duration of the traditional British cuckoo season. It has been all they can do to silence the thing for the indoor scenes and keep it from going in the village shop.

'I'm Off'

But out-of-kilter birdsong is a mere chirrup from the range of things that only happen in Ambridge. There is an abnormally high incidence of 'seeing oneself out'. OK, we all see ourselves out from time to time when visiting the infirm or elderly, though we tend not to make such a song and dance about it; but in Ambridge, seeing yourself out seems to be obligatory. The act of seeing yourself out occurs independently of mood, but anyone who is in a bit of a strop will precede their explained exit with an '*If* you'll excuse me – ', followed by a pause.

There are certain allied phrases that are only used by people in Ambridge. No one outside of the village would conclude a conversation in which they have become annoyed with the words, 'Well, I'll bid you good day, then.'

Cassandra Calling

Another idiosyncrasy in Ambridge is that accidents are always presaged by most of the villagers, but the victim to whom the mishap will befall is invariably too stupid to see it coming. For example, the slack on the steering of the Fergie was well flagged up before poor Jaaaarn took it for a spin. Whenever someone says, 'You need to mend that **** before someone falls in it/eats it/chokes themselves to death, etc.', you know that the urgent repair will not be carried out and the predicted calamity will duly materialise.

In a similar vein, people in Ambridge take a long time to ask the most obvious questions. Dayveed quite obviously knew who had been trashing the GM crop, but Roooooth took a day or so to tackle him about it.

Anno Domini

Old age certainly happens in Ambridge – in a big way. People carry on toiling, and are clearly expected to do so, in a way that probably wouldn't even occur in the Third World. The fact that Joe Grundy is pushing eighty in no way spares him from the rough and inarticulate edge of Clarrie's tongue for failing to do a major share of the housework and cooking, as well as a full day on the farm. Eddie treats him as if he's a skiving teenager when he demurs at the idea of getting up and doing the milking of a cold winter's morning.

Presumably connected with their outstanding longevity is the ability of all the old folk to retain their faculties. No one who speaks ever suffers from anything more than the occasional temporary bout of dementia and that seems to take on the seriousness of a minor summer cold. They might demonstrate rather loopy behaviour for a week or so (one remembers fondly the temporary madness of Martha Woodford, who was talking to ghosts, turning up in her nightie at dead of night to spring-clean the village phone box, etc.) but normal business is soon resumed. In the case of Martha, her full faculties returned to the extent that, a year or so later, she was taking a lead at a public meeting pontificating about abstruse areas of planning law.

The knack of reacquiring one's mental ability after previously appearing well on the road to senility, (sometimes referred to as *Saundersism*), was certainly enjoyed by the late Fat Man Forrest and has also been blessed upon Jeck Woolley. As we have so many old folk in Ambridge, it is something to look out for.

Surprised to be Young

But it's not only the elderly who behave in a unique manner, the youngsters have a tendency to forget that they are young and then suddenly behave in what they presumably imagine to be a stereotypical way. Take Wiwyerm Grundy, who only appeared to discover the existence of some 'mates' when his GCSEs were finished. Most people of his age, with no expectation of passing any exams, would have been out on the town *during* their exams, yet Wiwyerm's great mate Stuart hardly got a mention until this point. Then, true to *Archers* form, it was complete overkill with 'Stuart this, Stuart that' every other sentence.

PC World

Samples of political correctness discovered in Ambridge have been found to be several times higher than recommended levels for public safety. This leads to uniquely unusual reactions in matters such as health. Mrs Antrobus's reaction of joy on discovering that she would 'only' have to wait at least eight months for her cataract operation was so startling that we half expected her to burst into a rousing chorus of 'Things Can Only Get Better'.

Silence is Golden

Only in Ambridge is there a whole set of people who steadfastly refuse to speak when spoken to. Even Mrs Potter, a sprightly walking-frame scraping 250, managed to stay silent when she knocked over a load of tins in the village shop. This despite being shouted at in a patronising way by Beddy Tugger, a woman who generally has to wait a considerable time before finding anyone sufficiently far down the social order to warrant being patronised by her.

Things which one would expect to emit a noise only do so when mentioned. Sheep in Ambridge only bleat at shearing time, in the same way that traffic only makes a noise when it is under discussion. Lynda Snell only suffers from hay fever when she is talking about it, but otherwise her nasal passages are crystal clear, even when the pollen count is at its highest.

Mundane Fads

People do things spontaneously but simultaneously without any apparent co-ordination. For example, all of a sudden everyone seemed to be eating pasta. It was not as if it was National Pasta Day or Fettucini Fortnight. People, after nearly half a century of virtual pasta-free living, simply decided they could no longer live without the stuff and it was two fingers to the honest British spud. Peggoi even described pasta with vegetables as 'a treat'.

Sorted

Ambridge folk are very 'can do' people, which is the only plausible explanation for the enthusiasm with which they all talk of getting things 'sorted'. It is a verb much over-used in the village but everyone is just as likely to use it regardless of creed, colour, age or presumed vocabulary size. If you concentrate very hard during a conversation between, for example, the Dog Woman and Joan Pargetter you could be forgiven for thinking you were listening to a sound-track from *Brookside*. Even Siobhan Doctor's-Wife was using the word after being in Ambridge for five minutes. There is nobody who doesn't 'sort' things and the word comes up a dozen times per episode.

Urghh

The principal unique feature of Ambridge, for which we should never cease to give thanks, is that only in that village can there be such a high density of people upon whom you would wish to unleash a firing squad.

From the Cutting-room Floor II
The First Mrs Blandvoice Calls at Glebe Cottage

It is a perfect summer's day and Ambridge's winter birds are in full cry. The First Mrs Blandvoice (Quasimodette) has knocked at the door of Glebe Cottage, door bells being at something of a premium in Ambridge. The door opens and it is Damien, looking fully possessed.

Quasimodette: (*in a voice sounding as if she has a peg on her nose and a bag over her head – like a Virgin Trains on-board sound system*) Hello, is Mummy or Daddy at home?

Damien: My daddy is a test tube and my mummy is out looking for someone to bonk.

Quasimodette: Well, is your Uncle Phallustair at home?

Damien: Yes, he is.

Quasimodette: Will you go and get him for me, then, please?

Damien: Yes, I will.

An unsuspecting Phallustair comes to the door.

Quasimodette: Hello, Phally.

Phallustair: Oh, pooh ...

Rushes past Mrs Blandvoice, throws a saddle over Tibby the cat and disappears into the distance.

Quasimodette: Would you like to come and live with me?

Damien: Yes, I would.

Quasimodette: Well, come on, then, let's go.

Exit Damien and Quasimodette, hand in hooked claw.

From Lemons to Lower Loxley
Joan Pargetter – Victim or Villain?

This was, of course, the title initially chosen by Joan Pargetter for her autobiography. Sadly, she has led such a painful life that it proved too traumatic an undertaking and she reverted instead to the make-believe world of a steamy novel. We thought we should examine her case, for she is indeed a complex character and much wronged.

Joan seems to have been in the grip of most of the available vices – alcohol addiction, gambling, lust and shopping. But these are all relatively recent problems. She has not always had such an addictive personality. When her beloved husband, Gerald, swept her off her feet with a dead fox to put round her neck, she was as happy as Larry Lovell. But since his death, she has cut a lonely figure. Upper-class twit and former ice-cream and swimming-pool vendor Nigel was at first a doting son with a strong sense of filial loyalty. But, alas, the poisonous Lizzie has gradually turned him against his mother, taking advantage of his single-figure IQ to manipulate him at will. There is no question but that she has caused the decline in her mother-in-law via a process of ritual humiliation.

If your daughter-in-law moved into your home and then

suggested selling it off as a time-share, you would probably be incredulous. Yet this is exactly what Elizabeth was perfectly happy to consider as a means of realising some cash. After all, the girl has hardly done a day's proper work in her life, unlike her mother-in-law, who has toiled for many arduous years on the stage.

Joan has had a number of financial problems, something that could happen to any of us. These seem to have been caused by some difficulty she had in predicting which cards would be dealt in a couple of innocent card games and also in knowing against which number the ball was going to stop on the roulette wheel. If Elizabeth was not such a carrot-crunching yokel, she might have been to a casino herself. Then she would realise that these things just aren't that easy to predict. As anyone knows, if you fall off a horse, the best thing to do is to get straight back on, so if you get it wrong at the Black Jack table, you should go back and try again.

Elizabeth made a terrible fuss when one of Joan's financial advisers from the Spanish casino turned up at Lower Loxley to enquire about the settlement of an invoice. She then demonstrated her own selfishness by berating Loopy Nigel when, in a temporary moment of sanity and lucidity, he prevented his mother from selling a portrait of the much lamented Gerald.

The idea of writing a novel showed great resourcefulness, but the encouragement from her son and daughter-in-law has been non-existent. Her main problem with this project has not been lack of imagination and artistic creativity, which she has in abundance, but lack of technical resource.

Strangely, Lower Loxley does not seem to have a typewriter lurking in any dusty attic and she has been banned from using the office's one computer. It is also rather odd that there is only one computer, because in most businesses they are replaced on a regular basis, thus freeing up an old machine, which would have been fine for some simple word-processing. Joan's solution to the problem was unfortunately her only error of judgement. To recruit one of Ambridge's principal gossips – office cleaner and convicted criminal Jailbird Carter – as scribe was never going to be ideal.

Joan has a healthy dislike of Ellie May, which she regards as a Jersey Cow – not unreasonably given the facts, i.e., its brownness and general Jersey cow-like properties. This beast is symbolic of a more deep-rooted problem in that Nigel and Elizabeth have regarded it as a child substitute whereas Joan has always made it clear that she would prefer the patter of tiny feet to the splatter of Jersey pats.

Certain characters are bestowed with rather striking idiosyncrasies, and in Joan's case it is the tendency to disappear. 'Mummy's gone without saying anything, and I'm very worried about her,' says Loopy Nigel with monotonous regularity. The reason for this is that if your relatives spend all their waking hours making it clear to you that you are unwelcome, you probably deem it unnecessary to make a big announcement when you want to go away.

A particularly distressing feature of Joan in recent years has been the gradual reduction in her hitherto admirable class consciousness. It has always been a joy to behold her guiding any Lower Loxley visitor who is not wearing a tie firmly but politely in the direction of the tradesmen's entrance. The fact that this includes all the management fascists who turn up to 'bond' at their conference centre is particularly sensible. The idea that you can't bond when you are wearing a tie is clearly ludicrous.

Sadly, Joan has taken to lusting after the workmen who are a perpetual feature of Lower Loxley, offering them tea and discovering that they are all part-time art critics. Her decision to invite the builders to an art preview was somewhat out of character but, of course, well judged. There was a brief period during 1999 when even Loathsome Lizzie was forced to concede that Joan had a superior grasp of what was artistic than she herself possessed. This occurred when well-known art critic and Brian Sewell sound-alike Jeck Woolley congratulated her on the idea of displaying pictures on builders' scaffolding. It was typical of the woman that she refused to take credit for it and said that it was Elizabeth's idea as well.

The year 1999 was an important year for Joan, because she suddenly remembered she had a daughter. Camilla had barely been mentioned in living memory but, just in the nick of time, when the concrete overcoat boys were gathering, Joan went to Camilla and tapped her for a couple of grand. The existence of Camilla raises some important questions. Not only do she and her husband, James, never visit, hardly unusual in Borsetshire, of course, but Camilla never seems to have laid claim to a share in the family pile at Lower Loxley. James, of course, would not be permitted to enter Ambridge while Jamie Perks resides there since no two people with the same name can ever coexist. This incidentally explains why James Bellamy can never visit his grandma or other relations.

At the time of writing it is unknown whether the dreaded birth of Pargetter twins will go according to plan. But it seems inevitable that Joan will be denied her proper grandmotherly rights once they are born. More likely, Elizabeth will demand that Joan moves from Lower Loxley on the basis that the house is too small. Meanwhile Joan has been reduced to knitting baby clothes, which has caused an obscene level of sniggering between Foghorn and Elizabeth. Foghorn, a most un-Christian woman, clearly feels that she has a monopoly on nauseating cosiness and is viciously scathing of any grandmotherly gestures from Joan.

Joan's idea of commissioning Jailbird to knit something on her behalf seemed eminently sensible; indeed Marks & Spencer make a pretty reasonable living out of offering what is in effect the self-same service. So why people were outraged that Joan should pass this off as her own work seems incomprehensible. Is there suddenly a new law requiring us to state whether we have bought or made the gifts we choose to give?

In recent times Joan has found some solace in the friendship of a silent man called Louis. This she richly deserves. Our only real hope for her is that she may remember in the nick of time that Lower Loxley belongs to her and reclaim it to enjoy in her dotage. The prospect of Nigel, Elizabeth, Dum Sim and Ying Yong living in a council house with Ellie May is positively lip-smacking.

Quiz Four
Medical Matters

Questions

1. With which medical man was Caroline shacked up before meeting Robin Vetvicar-Stokes?

2. Dr Poole took over from whom as the village doctor?

3. To what non-medical organisation did Dr Death belong apart from the cricket team?

4. How is it that you hear Mrs Potter before you see her?

5. Who must never be far from a public or private convenience?

6. From what disease, apart from being terminally ridiculous, did Walter Gabriel suffer?

7. Who was stricken by the 'Falling Sickness'?

8. Who had an ectopic pregnancy?

9. Who attempted to get Dr Death struck off for medical negligence?

10. Where is the nearest hospital to Ambridge?

Answers

1. Matthew Thoroughgood.
2. Dr McLaren.
3. The Sealed Knot.
4. You hear the scrape of her walking frame.
5. Mr Pullen.
6. Diabetes.
7. Brian Aldridge.
8. The ghastly Shul-ugh.
9. The excellent Mr Barraclough.
10. Borchester General.

Post-mortem

Painstaking research has revealed that listeners have been duped about the true reasons for the death of characters on several occasions over the years. Here are just ten instances where we are proud to be able to put the record straight.

1. Death of Handbag Hebden
What actually happened was that Mark was following one of those lorries with a message on the back reading, 'Well driven? Call 0800 123452'. He was so impressed by the impeccable driving exhibited by the driver of the vehicle that he immediately called the number on his mobile to log his congratulations. He was totally distracted and the rest is history.

2. Death of Grace Archer
Grace was in fact sniffing lighter fuel at the stables. Of course an Archer could never be thought to have done such a thing so a cover-up was launched.

3. Death of Ralph Bellamy
No one seemed to notice the coincidence that Lilian had

managed to chalk up two consecutively dead husbands in a very short space of time. Having tampered with an aircraft engine to dispose of Lester Nicholson, it was barely a challenge to swap Ralph's gout pills for something a little more lethal.

4. Death of Poll Doll

Now we know of Pat's mental instability, the case against the milk tanker should be reopened. The first Mrs Perks was just in the wrong place at the wrong time when Pat went into one of her schizoid rages. It was not helped by the fact that Poll Doll innocently began talking about sausages.

5. Death of Dan

While the records will always show that Dan was savaged by a sheep, the truth is that it was Elizabeth who forced him out of a car and made him confront the sheep. Despite the tendency of very old Archers to do very strenuous things, sheep-wrestling is no sport for a man in his nineties.

6. Death of Jack Archer

Peggoi has always been attracted to Jacks, but she became a bit of a killjoy with the late Jack. He was one of those people who liked a drink. Very much. Often. In large quantities. In other words, he was a very thirsty man. Peggoi drove him to a mental breakdown with her now legendary nagging. When he insisted on having the odd drink to be sociable, Peggoi had him incarcerated in a remote Scottish clinic where she had sold him for use as a guinea pig in germ-warfare experiments. He was never seen again. Peggoi is now a wealthy woman.

7. Death of Walter

This was very straightforward. His habit of saying 'Me old pal, me old beauty' was so irritating, even to his friends, that Pru knocked up a batch of lethal scones, the very thing that was eventually to cause her own demise. What goes around comes around.

8. Death of Charlie Box

This was an interesting one. The whole village was suddenly plunged into mourning some years ago over the death of someone whose name had never been heard to pass anyone's lips. In fact he was a fictitious character invented to enable the burying of one of 'The Disappeared' to take place without suspicion. Anarchists demand an immediate exhumation.

9. Death of Guy Pemberton

A fine example of murder by telephone. The Village Bicycle nagged him over the phone, encouraging him to do the dirty on his hard-working son. Thus when he had his fatal heart attack, she was nowhere near the scene.

10. Death of Doris

Peacefully smothered with a pillow by Shul-ugh in order to expedite the transfer of Glebe Cottage to her greedy possession.

Horrible Hayley – Angel of Death
Friend of the Elderly and Imminently Dead

Hayley Jordan has rapidly turned into one of those nauseating goody-goody characters who put us off our suppers. Thankfully we are now building up a more realistic picture of the true character behind that whining Brum accent.

Animal lovers everywhere will have been deeply upset by the appalling episode in early 1999 where Horrible Hayley turned up at Nightingale Farm with Phallustair Blandvoice in tow and proceeded to bury Mrs Antrobus's beloved Afghan Portia. In their enthusiasm, they just about remembered to kill the poor animal first. That they were prepared to bury a perfectly good dog was nothing short of scandalous, but why did it happen? The answer is startlingly simple. Hayley cannot go for more than a few months without a death to enjoy, and poor Portia was by way of an interim sacrifice.

Her behaviour since the death of Jaaaarn defies any kind of logic. Bereavement counsellors must have observed her with grim fascination to such an extent that next time some poor grieving city-dweller comes their way they can say, 'Ah, what you need to do is take up organic farming and sausage production. Never fails.'

She must be making a bob or two out of the whole business. To start with she got Jaaaarn's engagement ring without having to marry him. Frequent visits to Keeper's Cottage to see dear old murderer Uncle Tom must have been quite lucrative, as she pocketed the odd knick-knack while he rambled on about the length of his marrers.

Doubtless she has played a kind of Fagin role with the children on the rare occasions she remembers that she's meant to be a full-time nanny, sending them to their posh homes with a little 'shopping list' of valuables. She will have got a good wedge from Foghorn for administering the poison to Tom and Pru, after which she has really gone into overdrive. Rent-free accommodation at Nightingale Farm, gradually milking poor old Mrs A for the late Teddy's remaining guineas and a whole lot of free furniture from all and sundry.

You have to hand it to her, she keeps plenty of irons in the fire and for a while was concurrently conspiring to make herself indispensable to Mrs A while making a major bid for a back-door 'partnership' in Bridge Farm. We saw the real Hayley when she was rumbled, thanks to Helen. Tony for once in his life made a firm intervention to make sure Hayley remained no more than a 'hired hand'.

Despite her claims to the contrary, Hayley was desperate to get back in with a chance of grabbing hold of Bridge Farm and she did it in the most underhand way. Realising that Pat was away with the fairies, Hayley suddenly decided to pay her a visit. Pat was there surrounded by bottles of pills kindly donated by Smarmy Dr Tim, debating whether to take them. She was preparing to make her decision on sound medical grounds such as 'Ip dip sky blue', when she asked Hayley, 'Do you think I should take them?' Hayley, naturally delighted at being able to make a medical diagnosis, decided that, as Pat was not at that particular moment climbing the walls, it was unnecessary for her to take any medication. Luckily Helen came to the rescue, expressing surprise that Hayley had apparently become a doctor overnight and justly accusing her of 'worming her way back into the family when Mum's vulnerable'.

Whether she has any nannying qualifications is always open to question. No one will forget the time when she was heavily implicated in an attempt to disfigure young Peeeep with toxic face paint. Weeks have often passed by without any reference to the kind of things that nannies habitually do, like looking after children. Once in a blue moon she would be heard talking to some silent children with posh names like Arabella and Becky. She allegedly looks after a couple of noiseless children called Becky and Henry for their mother, Jose.

While these are the kind of name you would expect children with nannies to have, there is something not quite kosher about this. Jose is described as 'a working mother' who works rather odd hours and likes to pop back and see her children during the day. This would imply that she works nearby, yet there is clearly no scope to work in Ambridge unless she is alongside Tugger and Carter fighting over 'tractor work'.

Whereas most people would regard nannying as being somewhat vocational, Hayley seems to regard it as a fall-back for when she can't be indulging her primary passion, making sausages. Her reluctance to look after the angelic Jamie Peacock-Perks and give him little runs from his cage occasionally was only overcome when she was told in no uncertain terms that she could sling her hook from Bridge Farm.

She is certainly undermining the nannying profession. Most nannies claim they are grossly overworked and underpaid, yet Hayley has thought nothing of running a sausage empire and acting as a chauffeuse to Mrs A, and seems to find the nannying business mere child's play, so to speak.

Hayley has sought to rationalise the death of Jaaaarn and the thorny question of blame. She has come to the conclusion that the only person to blame is Jaaaarn himself, which is quite convenient as the poor chap has little opportunity to defend himself and Hayley herself may otherwise bear some responsibility for the whole business.

More recently Hayley has lurched into child-care in a big way. 'The more the merrier' was her highly irresponsible attitude when offered Damien, BSE Josh, and little Peeeep to look after as a job-lot due to the knee-capping of Foghorn. In Ambridge there appear to be no regulations about the child/carer ratio, and Dickensian standards rule.

If Hayley is to get her come-uppance, it will probably be brought about not only by her all-consuming greed, but by her insatiable desire for publicity. We have all been forced to stand by helplessly while she has taken over at funerals, performed in the Red Nose Day débâcle and thrust herself to the fore in any dreaded village production. We then had to suffer the embarrassment of her insisting upon talking to Radio Borsetshire on the subject of strawberries, edging out poor plodder Neil, who was trying in vain to broadcast some interesting facts. She then abandoned the children in her care in order to dress up as a strawberry for a cheap sales gimmick.

It is strange indeed that an urban dweller such as Hayley should become so obsessed with pig farming and it seems inevitable that she will continue to attempt to worm her way into a slice of the Bridge Farm pie. She has presumably had a long-term plan to marry Lancastrian Tommy and is clearly infuriated at the fact that he has taken his eye off the entrepreneurial ball in order to wage a crusade against triffids. The arrival on the scene of Kirsty has also queered the pitch. But you should never write off Horrible Hayley. We just have to hope that Helen will remain vigilant.

Future Agenda

There is little evidence of forward planning in Ambridge, but Anarchists believe there are some extremely significant issues about the future that make the millennium bug pale into insignificance in comparison. It is essential that someone gives some proper thought to this NOW.

Who is going to be speaking in twenty to thirty years' time? There are many people who are unlikely to be with us, unless they are refrigerated like Walt Disney. Phil, Foghorn, Mrs Antrobus, Jeck and Peggoi, Great-great-great-great Auntie Chris, Joe Grundy, Boring George, Joan and Bert for starters. There are plenty of people around in Ambridge, but it's important that more of them chip in here and there and start to pull their vocal weight. Otherwise one day we'll tune in and there will be thirteen minutes of silence, broken only by the cuckoo and, if it's winter, the unceasing breaking of sticks. Is it too late for Trudy Porter to find a voice? Isn't it time the Carter kids put their vocal cords in gear?

Archers Anarchists, willing to lend a hand with an almost Brownie-like zest, have considered a couple of likely scenarios for the future.

Look to the Fuchsia – The Woolley Empire

The death of Jeck Woolley in 2006 will see the arrival of a whole string of pretenders to the throne at Grey Gables. Higgs will emerge from behind a wall of chrysanthemums to claim that Jeck had bequeathed the whole place to him many moons ago. Various 'sons' will turn up, pretending to be love children. Peggoi, if still alive, will be completely gaga and will spend every waking hour telling her children (who will be visiting her on a rotational basis three times a day) how no one ever visits her. Tony will have been given power of attorney over Peggoi's affairs, but to his utter chagrin he will discover that canny Jeck had made sure that none of his wonga was going the Archer way.

This will be particularly devastating news to all at Bridge Farm, who will have borrowed heavily in anticipation of copping most of Jeck's pile. Carolide, the Village Bicycle, will be sitting smugly with the certain expectation that Jeck will have rewarded her for her years of toil at Grey Gables. But Jeck will have decided that since she owns the Dower House and half the Bull and is completely loaded anyway, she wants for nothing. He will therefore have left just two little keepsakes to her – the stuffed lynx and an urn containing Captain's ashes.

Jeck will have given a surprising amount of consideration as to who should inherit his numerous interests and his decisions will rock the village. The Grey Gables side of things, including the Country Park and Golf Course and Health Club, will all go to Trudy Porter, someone who has never been heard to complain once in all her life and who was already working for Jeck before Carolide arrived on the scene. This will create the wonderful position where Trudy finally becomes the Bicycle's boss.

But what of the village shop and the *Borchester Echo*? Hazel will get these and make a long overdue return to Ambridge. She will be furious that she hasn't inherited Grey Gables, but these two businesses will give her ample scope to cause local mayhem.

At fifty, Hazel will have lost none of her charm but will have developed a hard-nosed entrepreneurial streak. She will sell a half-share in the *Borchester Echo* to Matt Crawford and together they will relaunch the paper as a *Sunday Sport*-type publication. It will be full of stories of aliens landing on Lakey Hill and TFW indulging in three-in-a-bed sessions – in other words, business as usual.

The village shop will never be the same again. Villagers will have taken up the post office on the idea that they should 'Use it or lose it' and will have lost it. So far as the shop side is concerned, it will cease to be a general store and will become a kind of Ann Summers specialising in the occult. This will be greatly welcomed by the likes of TFW, Damien, Kate and Lynda. Jailbird Carter will be out on her ear, and Beddy Tugger is clearly not the right image for such a shop. Hazel will put the local dominatrix Siobhan Hathaway in day-to-day control as Manager.

Sadly, with the larger-than-life character of Jeck departed from the scene, Grey Gables will rapidly fail as a viable business. In a desperate effort to revitalise the place Trudy will enter into a disastrous experiment with Sean Myerson and it will be renamed Gay Gables. But despite the overwhelming enthusiasm for homosexuality in Ambridge, it will just continue to lose money.

It will be good old Matt Crawford who rides to the rescue. Matt, turning on the charm and his silver tongue, will make an offer to Trudy that she can hardly refuse. Matt will get the whole Country Park for a fraction of its true value, since no one will realise that he has already smoothed the way to ensure that he wins the necessary planning consent, even if it does have to be won on appeal. He's known as a very generous donor to party funds, which by now are much needed since trade unions were banned by the second Blair administration.

A whole new town is to be built where once roamed Captain

and where formerly the strains of the Tommy Croker Quartet could be heard. But it's not bad news for everyone. Three broken figures can be seen beating a path to the prefab office where the hard-hatted Matt is in conversation with his forewoman (Debbie Aldridge). It's none other than the One-eyed Monster, Neil Carter and Eddie Grundy. 'We hear there might be some bulldozer work going ... '

Wither the Bull?

It is a sad fact, but in all likelihood there is only one way for the Bull to go and that's further downhill. Sid will strangle himself as the result of an unhealthy contortion with a dumbbell and that will be the end of him. This will leave the Bull in the reluctant hands of Kathy, who hates customers and cooking, and the Bicycle, who never goes anywhere near the place nor seems to mind whether it succeeds or fails. But on the old kangaroo vine, news of Sid's death will filter through to Lucy, who will be back in Britain faster than you can say Qantas, and certainly faster than you can fly it.

Once she arrives on the scene she will really kick off big style. To her shock, amazement and chagrin, she will discover the existence of half-brother Jamie, by now a dapper teenage warrior, melting hearts in the village wherever he goes. To Lucy, 'half-brother' will mean just one thing – 'half-inheritance'. There will be a right old ding-dong between Lucy, Kathy and the Bicycle. Lucy will have high hopes of turning the place into an Aussie theme palace, specialising in Australian cuisine – about as appropriate as turning Harlow into an international heritage site. On the other hand, the Bicycle, who was once daft enough to allow herself to become godmother to Wiwyerm Grundy, will want to install Wiwyerm as new landlord at the Bull.

Wiwyerm's career as a gamekeeper will have been sadly cut short some while earlier when Matt Crawford and his mates, having had a generous quantity of sherbets, will have mistaken him for a pheasant and confined him to a wheelchair. He will have become the first non-geriatric disabled character in sixty years of Ambridge life. Unable to resolve the love-tug pub problem, the three women will turn to St Usha to help resolve matters. The fact that Usha will have a conflict of interest acting for three different interested parties in the same case will be rather unfortunate, but there is only ever one lawyer in *The Archers* at any given time, so tough. As we all know, the only people to make money in these situations are the lawyers. The Bull will therefore have to be sold to pay her fees.

To save the hassle, Usha will kindly agree to accept the Bull in full and final settlement, without prejudice, or maybe with a little bit. She will take over as landlady and licensee at the Bull, changing its name to the Viceroy. This would bring back many happy memories to Marjorie, except that she'd be long since dead, having suffered a fatal infection after finally trying to perform her own cataract operation.

Roy Tugger will be in two minds about the whole business. On the one hand he'll be delighted by the 'roy' bit in the pub's name though a bit iffy about the 'Vice'. But he'll also have some unease, recollecting that many years previously he'd been a co-conspirator with Messrs Spanner and Craven in the sending of free samples of dog excrement to Blossom Hill Cottage. Will he be banned from his local?

Ambridge never has a problem with assimilating other cultures or any form of minority, and not one word of objection will be raised to the name change or to the disappearance of Shires to be replaced by Kingfisher Lager. Even ageing Mrs High and Mighty Aldridge will be full of admiration at the flock wallpaper and the false ceilings. But the days of the 'all part of the friendly service' Bull we know and love will have given way to a new life of popadums and vindaloos.

GM Feud

In a village where every character appears to be genetically modified, it is perhaps unsurprising that the subject of GM food had been of so little interest many months after it was gripping the nation. The 'Ambridge Socialist', a North London-based movement that campaigns 'for a living wage in Ambridge: £4.60 an hour', actually approached Archers Anarchists seeking to find common cause in the perceived failure of the BBC to tackle the question of GM crops at Home Farm.

Their contention was that it was a Blairite conspiracy to silence any discussion on the matter. We duly considered the matter as carefully as we consider anything, which was rather half-heartedly, and came to the conclusion that while it was nice to know of the existence of 'Ambridge Socialist' we couldn't really go along with their philosophy. Not only do we consider that £4.60 per hour is far too much to pay the likes of Jailbird Carter and the Tuggers, but we rather like the idea of Brian Aldridge manufacturing triffids on a grand non-organic scale.

It would appear that we were worrying unnecessarily, for it was not long before the whole grisly business was being argued out among the great intelligentsia of Ambridge. The brains of such luminaries as Jailbird Carter and Beddy Tugger were soon going twelve rounds with those of Lancastrian Tommy, Neil and the One-eyed Monster.

But discussion over this issue has been sporadic even by the standards of Ambridge, where campaigns tend to blow themselves out like some kind of tropical storm. The first intimation that Brian was growing these crops came when Lynda Snell rumbled him. Brian managed to persuade her that what he was actually doing was trying to grow pollen-free crops so that her hay fever would become a thing of the past.

Poor Lynda swallowed this line for a while and unfortunately became the laughing stock of the nastier Ambridge folk. What was rather surprising was that for a time she most uncharacteristically ceased to raise any objection, whereas we would have expected one of her off-the-shelf (or trolley) campaigns to have emerged instantly.

Debbie, whose role in life is to take a contrary view to Brian and then be completely steam-rollered, has hardly expressed a view on the fact that Porton Down has come to Ambridge. Even Kate, who usually pauses between sponging off her parents just long enough to try to sever the hand that feeds her, barely broke sweat on the issue to begin with, although she is of course against it. Surely this is the kind of thing that would cause most of the alternative caravan club and dirty-plaited-hair brigade to turn up in force. Luther could have turned up to pay his maintenance for Phoebe, and Morwena the Witch should have descended with her Kazoo and middle-class accent.

Tony objects to everything Brian does on principle because it is Brian who always ensures that the chip on Tony's shoulder is kept firmly in place. But even Tony had never spoken about Brian's GM experiments until That Fisher Woman accosted him and said she was writing an article for the parish rag about the issue and knew that Tony had 'strong views about it'. How she knew is something of a puzzle, because Tony had never previously mentioned the subject. However, he readily agreed that he was dead against it and exclaimed, 'I can't understand why I'm the only one who's saying anything about it.' The answer is probably quite simple – they were all indulging in a similarly strong silent protest and nobody had noticed.

One might ask what on earth TFW is doing writing about GM food in her parish magazine. It's typical of the woman, who will talk about anything except church matters. She should be writing about hassocks and cassocks, and God and Baby Jesus, and how many angels you can balance on a pinhead.

Tony formed a strange alliance with Robert Snell, who declared himself 'livid' that he found himself buying GM products in supermarkets without knowing about it. For someone who has always allowed his beloved 'Lyndybottom' to run all the village campaigns, it was rather strange that he should be so fired up by this.

A meeting in the village hall was convened to discuss Brian's crops. This was rather ambitious, since no one, bar Tony, TFW and Robert, apparently minded. Most people would have welcomed a few multi-headed animals and talking crops in Ambridge. But the antis knew what they were about as Lynda suddenly remembered that she was against it after all and Lancastrian Tommy decided to back his father's line for once in his life.

Brian Monsanto Aldridge seemed to be allowed a massive amount of air time to tell us how wonderful his triffids were going to be and how beneficial they would be for the Third World. WD 40 manufacturers must have felt their noses well out of joint, since they had hitherto been under the impression that they were the official sponsors of *The Archers*. All credit to Brian, he did such a good job that most of us were positively drooling at the idea of GM food, all but manning the barricades at supermarkets to demand double GM rations. Not since mobile phones were discovered to enhance our memories had such an excellent PR campaign been mounted.

The public meeting was predictably biased against the wonders of GM crops, but then protest meetings do tend to be attended by protesters rather than the satisfied and enthusiastic majority. There was no sign of all the silent people from Glebelands and the council houses, who were doubtless sitting comfortably at home stuffing E numbers down their throats like there was no tomorrow.

Lancastrian Tommy dismissed the few GM supporters at the meeting as 'wrinklies', a disparaging comment which must have caused great offence to the prune industry. Opinion diverged largely along class lines, the village riff-raff generally supporting Tony, as did a sprinkling of middle-class liberals such as Lynda and Robert.

A couple of exceptions were former trade unionist turned cyclops Mike Tugger, who seemed maniacally in favour of all things GM for reasons not totally unconnected, we suspect, with the large amount of 'tractor work' he was getting from Brian at the time. He reckoned it was 'the future of farming'. And Jailbird reckoned she would prefer to eat triffids than starve, on the basis that she couldn't afford poncy organic food.

Why did TFW chair the public meeting? It was very unclear under whose auspices the whole thing was being run – and where was George Barford, chairman of the parish council and the obvious person to take the chair? At the meeting that we were privileged actually to hear rather than hear about, much talk was made of Kate's heckling of her father. Strangely we didn't hear a sound – perhaps the microphones were faulty. The only heckling we did hear came from the broad Lancastrian vocal cords of Tommy, who bellowed out 'too raaaaght' a couple of times while his father was speaking.

The village was, of course, on tenterhooks to hear on which side of the great debate would fall the weighty intellect of Sidney Perks. Pub landlords generally hold a somewhat questionable place in society as the nation's opinion-formers. This despite the fact that their conversation is too often confined to a riveting account of the timed comings and goings of their regulars, coupled with an analysis of whether or not the male members would find themselves in the 'doghouse' as a penalty for their visit to their establishment. We were not disappointed when, shortly after the public meeting, Sid opined that most people 'couldn't give a monkey's'.

Things got rather lively when a group of helpful people kindly turned up to Home Farm to harvest Brian's GM crop. Brian, in whose mouth butter would not normally melt, got a bit annoyed because it wasn't quite ready for harvesting and he'd been saving it up to make sheaves of triffids for the harvest festival. He described the harvesters as a 'bunch of tree-hugging anarchists'. We assume he wasn't referring to us, because we don't like trees. We think they should all be cut down to make newspapers.

The good thing about the whole incident was that Dayveed weighed in and got a black eye for his busybodiness. The BBC managed to milk this story for weeks with the finger of suspicion being pointed firmly in the direction of spoilt wild-child Kate. The Radio 4 programme *Feedback* gave a lot of coverage to outraged people who felt that the protesters were being misrepresented as violent people who punch people like Dayveed.

As far as we are concerned, no one needs an excuse to punch Dayveed. Apparently, people who trash triffids are really nice people who, when not doing this public service, can be found helping old people across the road, a service they tend to provide without the cover of balaclavas.

It was obvious that the voluntary threshers were going to include people we knew, although, given their characters, it was rather incredible. When the Fuzz turned up at Bridge Farm the day after the Single Wicket Competition to arrest Lancastrian Tommy, the amazing truth of the whole affair suddenly dawned upon Anarchists throughout the nation.

As Tommy was being interviewed by his solicitor and the police, we were all beginning to regret the shortage of special-needs teachers in our schools. The poor bloke could hardly open his mouth without almost incriminating his co-conspirators. Those of us from outside Ambridge, with ready access to the media and national newspapers, realised the coincidence that Tommy had been pulled in at the same time as Prince Charles was launching a tirade against triffids.

From that point onwards it was quite obvious that, whoever else was made to carry the can for the Home Farm harvest, the other two miscreants were HRH and TFW. The latter had conveniently gone on her walking holiday until things had blown over. It is not the first time that royalty has turned up in Ambridge, but it was certainly game of our future king to throw himself into village matters with such enthusiasm.

The reactions to Tommy's deeds were fairly predictable. We had Mrs High and Mighty Aldridge going around on a horse that must have been well over 100 hands in height. In the same breath she would say that she was going to make Tony (whom she blamed for the whole thing) 'wish he'd never been born', *and* how keen she was not to divide the family.

This was rather unnecessary since, on the first point, Tony, knowing what his older sister is like, probably began wishing he'd never been born the moment he emerged from under the stork. On the other count, the Archer family is actually manufactured to divide, modelled on the traditional Kit-Kat style of breaking into two or four parts on demand. Jennifer got herself so wound up about the whole business that she told Pat that her family was barred from Home Farm.

Helen, who could doubtless see excellent marketing prospects for triffids, thought Tommy had behaved like an idiot – a statement on which she could have saved her breath had she added ontology as an option in her studies. She tried to equate the crime with the great sausage betrayal by describing it as a case of 'act now, think later, just like with Hayley and the sausages'.

Pat, who had gone from bonkers to Boadicea in the space of about a week, rather took Tommy's side, saying that 'at least he cares about something'. The possibility that this could excuse every criminal ever to have walked the earth seemed to have escaped her.

Kate was full of admiration for Tommy's daring and actually called round to say so. The prospect of these two cohabiting together would be a delight. Since the average IQ level in the village would suggest that most of the inhabitants must have married their cousins fairly regularly throughout the ages, it shouldn't be too much of a problem.

Tommy was bursting with Lancastrian pride at his principled stand. Described in the *Borchester Echo* as an 'Eco Warrior', he repeated his vow not to 'grass on my mates' – a rather over-familiar way of describing Prince Charles. Like all people with principles, he had great difficulty with the concept of a 'full and frank apology', the price demanded by Mrs High and Mighty. He could have taken a leaf from the book of the late Jaaaarn, who was always rather adept at compromising his principles.

Peggoi weighed in with her two-penneth and, being a moral upstanding woman nowadays, was aghast to find that she had washed the overalls that Tommy had been wearing on the night of his daring deed, including traces of Dayveed's eye no doubt. She was all for grassing him up – an act which would have done wonders for family unity.

Peggoi has developed a unique and utterly futile solution to family conflict. This takes the form of organising and enforcing a big family celebration just as people are at their most daggers-drawn. Having tried it during the sausage business, she set about arranging a similar event to celebrate Jeck's eightieth birthday, bang in the middle of the GM conflict. Tommy, whose mental footwork is modelled on a tortoise, excelled himself for once by describing his nice old granny as 'The Gestapo'.

Tommy, with true Lancastrian grit, had no fear of going to prison but became rather concerned that the British justice system might include a fine that had to be paid in pigs. This was a notion that Mrs High and Mighty Aldridge rather cruelly sowed in his pedestrian mind. Once he'd had a taste of porridge when his bail was refused, Thomas felt somewhat different. He complained to Tony that he felt lonely in his cell, and then rather contradicted himself by saying that the occupant of the adjacent cell was being sick all night. As a qualified projectile vomiter, he ought to have felt he'd encountered a kindred spirit.

The trial of Tommy was destined to last for an age once the politically correct St Usha arrived to take up his defence. Seeing some fat fees on the horizon, she cheerfully encouraged him to claim that landing one on Dayveed could clearly be justified on the basis that the Bridge Farm pigs were in imminent danger of attack from Brian's triffids. Twelve good men and bonkers could surely be found in Borsetshire to go along with this line. St Usha was in her element, becoming an expert on GM issues overnight and wheeling out all manner of right-on loonies to slag off our beloved triffids.

One of the casualties of Lancastrian Tommy's illegal exploits was that the 'y' at the end of his name mysteriously disappeared. Spontaneously, all kinds of people began calling him 'Tom'. We can only assume that the y became detached while he was running away from the scene of the crime.

Perhaps the whole episode over GM crops gave a clue to the usually concealed politics of people in Ambridge. Anyone who was New Labour would agree with Tony Blair that triffids should be regarded as 'The people's triffids', and that having several heads is all part of 'New Britain'. The problem is that in Ambridge all the characters who seem to take that line are the most likely people to be Conservatives, such as Brian and Jennifer. Other pro-triffid people like Cyclops Tugger and Jailbird Carter would probably vote BNP because they think St Usha is taking their jobs. One can understand their point of view, as it is patently obvious that the only obstacle to Jailbird becoming a highly paid solicitor is the presence of Usha. But, above all, the whole GM business has served to 'out' yet another Archer criminal in the form of Lancastrian Tommy – thug and vandal.

Quiz Five
MENSA Level

With a couple of exceptions to save embarrassment, we really are talking anorak *at the very least here, if not* parka. *If you can answer more than 50 per cent of these questions you have our very deepest sympathy, and we would only remind you that new cures are discovered for the most challenging afflictions and conditions almost daily.*

Questions

1. On what occasion were we introduced to Marjorie?
2. Who was the previous owner of Blossom Hill Cottage before St Usha?
3. Who would die for the Queen?
4. What position of minor importance did Neil take over from Mike Tugger when Mike left Brookfield?
5. What was the name of the dog with whom the Village Bicycle arrived in Ambridge?
6. Jeck Woolley on one of his thrift binges decided to introduce a cheap brand of products to the village shop. This soon petered out when the villagers didn't like them. What was the brand name?
7. What was the name of Loopy Nigel's former enterprise in the retail sector?
8. What was the name of Lilian's first husband?
9. What did Foghorn say when she learned that her gay son, Kenton, had married?
10. What was the stage name of Jolene Rogers?

Answers

1. She came to address the WI on the subject of Afghan hounds.
2. Lilian.
3. Captain.
4. Union Rep.
5. Leo (Great Dane).
6. Pleasant Valley.
7. Mr Snowy (ice-creams).
8. Lester Nicholson.
9. 'Better get that pie out of the oven.'
10. The Lily of Layton Cross.

That Fisher Woman
The Case Against

No one would ever accuse Archers Anarchists of being anything other than reasoned and balanced, so it may come as a surprise that we have not felt able to accord a Christian acceptance to 'The Reverend' Janet Fisher, despite her presence in Ambridge for a few years. It should be pointed out that the epithet 'That Fisher Woman', which we prefer to abbreviate to a more friendly 'TFW', was originally coined by Joe Grundy, who described her thus before she had so much as set webbed foot in the village.

Some of the more right-on listeners doubtless think our objections to TFW are rooted in the fact that we are the kind of people who wish to prop up the bar at the MCC without hearing discussion of knitting patterns. Nothing could be further from the truth. The author has been known to create several woollen scarves and, having little more than a passing interest in cricket, would not be unduly concerned if the bar of the MCC took to admitting man-eating tigers. No, the letter-columns of our newsletter are regularly peppered with reasoned arguments to suggest that TFW is a sham and an impostor, and this is the case that deserves examination.

No Suitcase

TFW is an androgynous creature who, in common with many others, arrived in Ambridge totally devoid of any past. Ambridge arrivals are like escaped prisoners of war in that they turn up with just the rudimentary documentation that will suffice to get them into the community. In TFW's case, she came armed with nothing more than a dog collar and a middle-class accent.

Resistance is Futile

Before she arrived there was a healthy campaign waged by the neo-fascist section of the Church of England in Borsetshire. Peggoi Mitford-Woolley was one of the main driving forces behind the resistance to a beskirted vicar. She was ably supported by Derek Fletcher, a silent resident from Glebelands, who had never previously come so close to speaking. A less able couple of supporters were the late unlamented Fat Man Forrest and village idiot Bert Fry. You can add to that the completely useless support of Joe Grundy, who, as a devout Methodist, was rather disqualified from having an opinion. The fact that poor Joe doesn't get to the chapel as often as he ought should not be held against him and can be explained by the complete absence of a place of worship rather than any weakness of will on his part.

The key promoter of TFW was, needless to say, the awful Shul-ugh, who simpered on in her sanctimonious way and paved the way for her arrival. An extremely unholy alliance rapidly developed between Britain's most promiscuous churchwarden and the new vicarette. TFW was later to repay this loyalty in spades when Shul-ugh casually bedded the village doctor, cheated on her boyfriend, Phallustair, and one of her best friends, St Usha, and then coolly demanded a church wedding.

Once TFW arrived, resistance crumbled at an alarming pace. Most of the atheist villagers were pleased to see that organised religion in Ambridge had given way to a kind of pagan social work. It was clear that the only people who truly cared would be those who had a real involvement in the church. TFW cunningly picked these off one by one.

Phil Archer never gives a toss about who's in charge at St Stephen's as long as he can continue to be the organist. He's happily tickled the ivories through the reigns of numerous clergy. Music at the church has always been important to him. There is apparently a full-size cathedral organ in the church and a choir of King's College standards which seems to be comprised not only of silent characters but of non-mentioned ones.

And all this is achieved without the expense of a choirmaster. Allegedly the unseemly shenanigans at Westminster Abbey involving the sacking of the choirmaster were all based upon the premise that if Ambridge could produce perfectly good music without one, then surely Westminster could as well.

Derek Fletcher had fought a strong rearguard action against the ordination of women, but eventually even he had to accept that the impact he achieved by speaking out at public meetings in the village was greatly undermined by not having a voice. His continued silence should not, however, be taken as satisfaction with the new order and were he ever to be granted the power of speech things might be very different.

The most ridiculous capitulation to TFW acceptance was that of Bert Fry. He was wandering around the village telling anyone who would listen, which was generally nobody, of his great aversion to the imminent arrival of a vicarette. Then, on her arrival, she went up to him with a greeting along the lines of, 'Hello, you must be Bert Fry,' and he never looked back. It says something for the state of the Church today that the village idiot is deemed to be churchwarden material but when his running mate is Shul-ugh that really says it all.

To her eternal credit, Peggoi Woolley has remained vaguely hostile to the whole TFW 'project', as modern commentators would describe it. She has to travel some distance for her Sunday worship, since TFW seems to have muscled in on most of the surrounding parishes, such as Penny Hassett and Darrington. Thus All Saints', Borchester, seems to have her custom for the time being. Peggoi has rather let herself down by attending some of the pagan rituals, such as the bizarre funerals of Jaaaarn, Fat Man and Pru Forrest, presided over by TFW.

Fisher Fraud

As usual, it has fallen to Archers Anarchists to provide the most informed analysis of the scandals of TFW. We have the good fortune to boast at least three bona fide be-collared clergy among our ranks. Thanks to the diligent research by some of these experts, together with that of some lay God-botherers, we have been able to drive a coach and horses through the current regime at St Stephen's – about as close as Ambridge gets to public transport nowadays.

Several people have had the common sense to check in *Crockford's Clerical Directory*, only to find that there is no entry therein for a Janet Fisher. You might have thought that Bishop Cyril would have taken this basic step himself, rather than assuming that anyone who swans into his bishopric sporting a reversed collar and clutching the good book is a kosher cleric.

We have yet to discover why she is passing herself off as a proper vicarette. Is it to get easy access to the communion wine? Certainly she doesn't seem to be a frequent visitor to the Bull or even to the Pink Cat. She seems to have very little sense of duty when it comes to ministering to the sick, troubled or bereaved. This is hardly a full-time job in Ambridge, where illness has generally been something of a rarity, yet there have been a number of notable absences on the part of TFW when the grim reaper has been anywhere involved.

The late Mrs Barraclough, who was murdered by Dr Locke, was not visited by TFW. Indeed TFW was heard to mutter something like, 'I must find time to get over and see her' shortly before Mrs B's death, only to miss the boat by a couple of lethal injections. When Jaaaarn did his handbrake turns on the Fergie it was a long while before TFW showed up at Bridge Farm to comfort the bereaved, and the Health and Safety mob were several days ahead of her.

Mad 'n' Bad

TFW has done some very peculiar things that should really have resulted in her being sectioned indefinitely under the Mental Health Act. At the 1999 Palm Sunday Service she actually brought a donkey to the church. Her explanation that it was what Jesus was riding on Palm Sunday was completely unsustainable. By the same token she would have to flood the church to emulate the walking-on-water business, employ all the 'tractor work' whingers (workers in the vineyard parable), beat up a passer-by (good Samaritan) and buy up Borchester Cash and Carry (feeding of the 5K). And if she then got stuck in to the Old Testament it really doesn't bear thinking about – Mike Tugger would really have to be on his guard when she got to 'an eye for an eye'.

TFW is no lover of the country or its ways. She conspired with loony Bert Fry to drive out a bunch of bats from her belfry despite the fact that they are a protected species. It was a particularly un-Christian act to vilify bats who were happily living in belfries in times when the very idea of installing women vicars would have landed you in the Tower of London.

Fat Man Forrest was justifiably outraged by what they were doing, but unfortunately he had reached that age where the only words that would come out whenever he opened his mouth were, 'Oi, want to see moi Pru.' This was unfortunate because, instead of resulting in TFW being hauled before the courts, it just meant that some do-gooder would cart him off to the Laurels.

Keeping Christianity at Bay

One accusation that can never be levelled at the door of TFW is that of trying to spread Christianity around the village. She very rarely speaks of religion, lending weight to the notion that she is indeed a fraud. With typical modesty (TFW is the kind of woman who, if she were a nun, would wear a Day-Glo wimple), she defined 'the key to being a successful vicar' as 'knowing when not to interfere'. If ever there was a cop-out then this must be it, the perfect justification for perpetual indolence.

Good Friday 1999 was a bit of an eye-opener in Ambridge. TFW, with a rare bit of Christian symbolism, had bullied some of the Ambridge menfolk into carrying what she described as a 'replica wooden cross' from Darrington to Ambridge. One might ask what a wooden cross could possibly be a replica of? But it is also questionable whether there was much to be gained by asking people like Neil Carter, his back always bent with toil, to carry a heavy lump of wood around. People like Kathy Perks absolutely lapped it all up. 'She's so human for a vicar,' she drooled, and then by implication made the point that so many of us have felt for ages when she said, 'I'm glad she's making such a feature of Easter this year.' Easter does tend to be quite a big event in most Christian calendars.

Easter Day saw a typically off-the-wall sermon from TFW. She started off reasonably enough with the usual vicarly stuff about remembering the less fortunate rather than stuffing yourself with chocolate. Nothing wrong with that, unless you happen to be a Cadbury's employee. She seems to have a bit of a thing about chocolate because she gave it up for Lent, although she carefully avoided mentioning where her chocolate budget might have been reallocated.

Since thousands of British troops were engaged in NATO attacks on Serbia and the TV screens of our nation were full of harrowing footage of Kosovan refugees, we quite expected that TFW might encourage us to turn our thoughts in that direction. But not a bit of it. TFW wanted the people of Ambridge to cancel Third World debt and twin with an African village, and she had not a single word to say about the crisis facing Europe.

What exactly would be involved in this bizarre twinning practice was unclear. Presumably the main thing would be yet another place name in parenthesis on the 'Ambridge welcomes careful drivers' notice as you enter the village. As Ambridge doesn't really welcome anyone, it is already rather superfluous.

Also, would we have to endure the prospect of sanctimonious busy-bodies like Shul-ugh setting off for Africa armed to the teeth with Bibles and peace quilts? Or could we look forward to the already cosmopolitan village of Ambridge developing an African quarter and a source of cheap labour to lower further the employment chances of the Carters and Tuggers? It might be quite a good thing after all.

Having asked everyone to think about the Third World at a time when they should have been thinking about the second one, TFW then presided on Easter Monday at a pagan ceremony of the most vulgar nature. During this sinister ritual, children were told to stick two fingers up to the starving and were then forced to roll perfectly good free-range eggs down the slopes of Lakey Hill.

Holidays for the Hungry

TFW frequently displays a rather individual approach to the world's problems and in many cases her solutions are quite bizarre. Clearly eaten up by the problem of Third World debt, she suddenly had a brainwave that would solve the problem at a stroke. She decided to go on a walking holiday to Cologne. Such is her Svengali-like influence on some of her parishioners that she even managed to entice the Hindu St Usha to go with her.

Even the definitely non-cerebral Beddy Tugger felt moved to question whether Usha and TFW walking around would actually 'make any difference', a view echoed by the village elder, Phil Archer. This was obviously a naive question, as we all accepted that this selfless act of going on holiday would fill hundreds of thousands of empty bellies. Given all the pleasant walks that one could embark upon, however, the idea of walking from Birmingham to Cologne could have been considered a rather peculiar choice.

It does, moreover, open a whole new range of opportunities to solve other ills of the world in a similar manner. If we regard a 400-mile walking holiday as sufficient to write off Third World debt, we could confidently assume that an earthquake of say ten on the Richter scale could comfortably be compensated for by a couple of weeks in Butlins. An individual personal tragedy could, of course, require nothing more than a day off work on the part of some well-meaning third party. Even Armageddon could be seen off by a three-week cruise. Fat Clarrie was obviously thinking along the same lines when she commented that, if it would clear her own debts, she'd be perfectly happy to walk barefoot.

Not everyone is prepared to go along with TFW's schemes. Jailbird Carter has rapidly earned a reputation as the conscience of Ambridge ever since she was jailed for aiding and abetting an armed robber and absconding from prison. Remember it was Jailbird who let the rather scrawny cat out of the bag when she said at a public meeting, 'We all know why Dr Locke left the village, don't we?' So, too, it was Jailbird who said that she was not having any of the Jubilee Millennium Project because she didn't believe in ending Third World debt – people should pay their debts.

Such a politically incorrect view would obviously be given little quarter in the PC capital of the universe, but she was not entirely alone. Peggoi 'Call me old-fashioned if you will' (no, you're just a boring old trout, Peggoi) took the view that TFW should be looking after the needs of her parishioners. She described TFW's approach as 'short-sighted' and Jeck was certainly not prepared to support it. More significantly so did Bert Fry, adding 'quite a lot of people feel the same way'. Unfortunately they were the silent majority, a huge and largely impotent force in Ambridge. It might have been thought that Bert would carry some weight as a churchwarden, but he was clearly overridden by the ghastly Shul-ugh.

TFW took her holiday at a time when there were at least three people in Ambridge in dire need of succour. We had Pat with her sausage-induced breakdown, Joan Pargetter at risk of her life from El Ladbroke and Mrs Antrobus stumbling around the village asking to go to the bottom of the NHS waiting list.

So, once it became inevitable that TFW was going off on her holiday, that left the minor question of who was going to take church services during her absence? And here we enter the realms of something you just couldn't make up if you tried. Fornicator-in-Chief Shul-ugh Hebden-Blandvoice was given the job of leading a service. She has no qualifications to do so, unless going the distance with the village doctor behind the back of one of her best friends while supposedly going steady with someone else counts. Or maybe her qualification is simply her conviction – for taking and driving away?

There was a back-up to take the service in case Shul-ugh was rogering someone else that day, none other than pub quiz cheat Bert Fry. Was the Church of England safe in their hands? Apparently, if all else failed, Clive Horrobin would be let out on licence to do the honours.

The day the walking holiday began turned out to be one of the most revolting PC exhibitions ever heard on *The Archers*. Half the village were, of course, only too keen to get up at 5.30 a.m. on a Sunday morning and trundle off to Brum, where the walk was starting, to see off St Usha and TFW. All the usual suspects had turned up, including Shul-ugh and Roooooth, who was nauseatingly sycophantic about the whole business.

We were then subjected to 'live sounds' from the march. Being worthy, alternative and protesting in nature, this included a lot of obligatory whistles. It is a very strange phenomenon that protests of this kind always include copious quantities of whistles and it has never been explained whether ends are more or less likely to be achieved if accompanied by whistling. To most of us it would never occur that our complaints might be addressed more readily if we refrained from washing for a few days and then began whistling. Come to think of it, if this system were to be used in restaurants, it would probably improve the service no end.

TFW's feigned interest in world poverty is frequently exposed as the sham it is. At harvest time in 1998 she put on the most grotesque display of gluttony when she attended two harvest suppers in the same evening. By the time she arrived in Ambridge from Penny Hassett she was still trying to cram food down her throat, but reached the point where she could eat no more. So did she then begin to gather together what was left in order to re-enact the feeding of the 5K, loading up Eddie's van and departing for Africa? Did she, hell! No, she hid food in the font, aided and abetted by the other phoney God-botherer Shul-ugh, causing an outbreak of insect infestation in the church.

Not content with using St Stephen's as a larder, TFW has turned it into a tourist office with brochures and advertising. The only person to speak out against this outrage was the reliable Peggoi, but having taken her custom to All Saints' in protest at the very existence of TFW, she is not really in a position to do much about it.

Surprisingly and disappointingly, TFW's walking holiday may not have succeeded in curing Third World poverty. Numerous Anarchists have since reported back on trips, taken to various African countries, where they expected the population to now resemble Billy Bunter clones, but sadly it was not so.

Book Burning

Undaunted and refreshed, TFW stormed back to Ambridge with the devastating news that she intended to replace the hymn books. This was bad news for the traditionalists, as it obviously heralded the introduction of heathen happy-clappy practices designed to drive the last vestiges of Christianity from a village that is desperately crying for release from the ever-growing forces of darkness.

It should be noted that TFW increasingly has an attitude of complete contempt towards poor Bert and any of his views that belies her claims to be an authentic holy Joe. When the poor man stood out against her insistence on introducing these politically correct hymn books, TFW's Christian response was, 'Bert will have to put up and shut up.'

Tee Hee Hee

TFW has no genuine sense of humour. Her jokes are of the mirthless variety and she has the perpetual giveaway trait of the humourless, which is to tell people that she *has* got a sense of humour. This is a vital tool in the armoury of the mirthfully challenged since without being told we would never realise that our sides should by now be in danger of splitting.

Although TFW appears in the Top Ten of Anarchists' most loathed characters there is one reason that prevents her topping the poll – the continued existence of Shul-ugh.

Mr Davies's Diary

Mr Davies is a regular visitor to Brookfield, where he and his family avail themselves of the rather spartan Rickyard Cottage. While it is a mystery to many of us why anyone would want to holiday in Ambridge, it does take all sorts and who are we to question them anyway? As luck would have it, Mr Davies was so fraught during his last visit that he inadvertently left his diary behind and, joy, oh joy, it fell into Anarchist hands. It is not altogether polite to reproduce someone's private diary without their permission, but we are Anarchists after all and are happy to live life on the edge. So here are just a few excerpts from that fateful week.

Saturday
Arrived in Ambridge, via Borchester. We stopped in Borchester to shop and pick up a few provisions. As usual shopping there was a joy. We wanted to go to the Cash and Carry but we didn't have a card so went into the only other shop – Underwoods – which was completely empty apart from Jennifer Aldridge. Parking was easy, as there were only a couple of cars in the multi-storey – both from Ambridge.

As soon as we reached Ambridge we were stopped by paramilitary types

who fitted total silencers to the car. We filled in the usual paperwork with all
the declarations, agreeing not to use the village shop, the Bull or Grey
Gables, and above all not to speak while we were there.

It was nice to be welcomed on arrival by the excited silence of the
Brookfield dogs and cats. Dished out cotton-wool ear plugs to wife and kids
as we had to knock at the door of Brookfield Farmhouse to get the key to the
cottage. Even so, Mrs Foghorn caused a great deal of collateral damage to
our eardrums as she force-fed scones down our throats without even a
by-your-leave. We had been slightly taken aback when she first greeted us
because she shouted, 'What are YOU doing here?' at us, but then we
remembered that is the traditional Ambridge greeting – their equivalent of the
Eskimos' rubbing noses.

Rickyard Cottage hasn't changed. It's still like Stalag Luft III. We set to
work on the inventory. We've been turned over too many times before to get
taken in by that one. Just as well we checked. There in black and white was
listed a divided vegetable dish, but we searched high and low and it just
wasn't there. Bloody typical! All the other crockery and utensils were down
to the normal self-catering standard: tin openers that wouldn't be capable of
opening a paper bag and unmatching cups and saucers with more chips
than a large portion of McDonald's.

Sunday

Woken early by a strange Geordie whingeing sound that combined with an
indignant mooing noise to make it impossible for us to sleep. The place was
littered with dead hens and there seemed to be more foxes than cattle grazing
in the fields. That Foghorn woman really seems to have let the place slide.

We looked at the timetable for buses, only to find it was about forty-
eight years out of date. The last bus seen in Ambridge was apparently driven
by Walter Gabriel.

One bit of good news, we were able to buy newspapers for the first time.
Thanks to a silent but effective campaign by Robert Snell, the village is
awash with newspapers. They're all the rage and the local children are
silently making papier-mâché models like it's going out of fashion.

Apparently there are one or two televisions in the village now and a couple of the children have discovered a new programme called Blue Peter. Mind you, getting the newspapers from the village shop is a rather strange procedure as no one works there on a Sunday. You have to enter via a skylight and leave the money in an honesty box, which seems a bit risky in a lawless place like Ambridge.

No one spoke to us all day. Just seen a mattress go past the window, followed by a strange small creature with horns and a tail. That Shul-ugh must be visiting Brookfield.

The only other excitement of the day was a trip to St Stephen's, where we were just in time for a special evensong to celebrate St Lucifer. Sacrifices were made, mainly consisting of diseased cattle and a whole string of interesting pagan rituals was enacted. Afterwards we played an exciting game of 'Find the Food' in which various buffet items had been hidden all over the church. The vicarette seems quite a good sort – she didn't mention God or Jesus once, which is so refreshing in a church service.

Monday

Managed to get a copy of Things to Do in Borsetshire, which turned out to be an A6 sheet. We went for a walk up Lakey Hill, but it was rather embarrassing as you just couldn't move for copulating couples. The litter was appalling and I've never seen so many syringes, even in a hospital. The wife just didn't know where to look.

We went on to Hayden Barrow, which was almost as bad. It was like Piccadilly Circus, with earnest couples saying things like, 'Remember when we first came up here?' and 'Do you know, I don't think we've been up here since ****.' In fact it seemed that amnesia had broken out in a big way up there. Desperate for some peace and quiet, we went over to Marneys, only to find Foghorn's husband sitting there trying to break the world record for Large Homely Pack Lunch Consumption.

Tuesday

Had a chat to Foghorn, who told me that she was very conscious of giving her guests the 'full Brookfield experience', but I can see through all that claptrap. It is quite obvious to me that the whole family regards us as a damn nuisance and that we are just there as a cash cow because they are such inefficient farmers. In fact a cash cow is about the only one they've got left.

We decided to go to Grey Gables and that was a strange business. Apparently it was Fornication Day and the manageress of the place was taking part in a Bonkathon. The under-manageress was there, Trudy Porter, but she couldn't speak, which made things a bit difficult. There was a strange sort of Brum/Jewish old man called Jeck, who made noises that sounded like a cow in calf. The food was French nouvelle cuisine so it was two parts of sweet FA served up on a plate the size of a satellite dish. We wanted to have a swim in the health club, but it seemed that ever since the woman from the Bull stopped running it, they had forgotten to replace her. The water in the pool was a funny colour and there seemed to be dogs swimming about in it.

Wednesday

Went to the Bull for lunch and if yesterday was a bit odd, you should just hear this. As we set foot in the door, a woman let out an anguished wail and said, 'Oh, not a couple of customers,' She then said, 'I hope you don't want any food because I've got a child and I'm a teacher and I don't want to get my hands dirty cooking for scum like you.' Then a Brummie man who turned out to be her husband jogged in wearing a tracksuit and said, 'All part of the service we like to give in this traditional English village pub. Would you like a game of boules?'

What we actually wanted was a drink. The wife wanted half a lager, but Mr Perks said, 'What? Are you some kind of a homosexual or something? If you want lager you'd better go to the Cat and Fiddle. We don't want your sort here. It's Shires or nothing. All part of the service.' Eventually a silent woman called Freda rustled up a microwaved pie for us. There weren't many people in the pub, just a couple of blokes arguing about 'tractor work'.

Thursday

The wife's birthday. After the Grey Gables and Bull experiences I wasn't sure what to do but suddenly a strange woman called Peggoi appeared on the doorstep. Apparently she specialises in party enforcement. She can organise a party including a whole crowd of reluctant guests and everyone turns up with a face like a wet weekend saying how much they're enjoying themselves. So we went along with it and Mrs Davies said afterwards she hadn't enjoyed herself so much since she had mumps as a child. You should have been there for the chorus of 'Happy Birthday'— you could have heard a pin drop.

Friday

That's it, we're off. Today was the last straw. The cottage is just too poorly equipped to be able to cook proper meals, so we had asked if we could have breakfast with the people that the Brookfield crowd affectionately describe as 'The B&B scum'.

We went into Brookfield, where there were some ashen-faced guests, and it turned out that Foghorn had been knee-capped in some kind of demonic revenge attack. We weren't bothered about that, but we were less happy about the knock-on effect. It meant that Rooooooooooooooth was having to cook the breakfast.

Suddenly they announced that they'd had a cosy family meeting and had summarily decided to axe their B&B guests. An armed militia had been raised in the village and we were all escorted out, without even being allowed to take our possessions. Looting took place before our very eyes, with the village riff-raff, such as the Tuggers, Carters, Grundys and Horrobins, picking out what they wanted. Luckily we'd left anything valuable at home, but they were obviously delighted with all our dirty washing and flip-flops. As we left, we heard the sound of the eponymous bridge being blown up to keep out further visitors.

New in Town

It is always a bit of a hostage to fortune writing a chapter on newcomers to Ambridge. For those who have bought this book in an antiquarian bookshop for ninety euros, we could have included Dan and Doris and no one would be any the wiser. But at the time of writing it seemed worth paying homage to the most recent characters to enter the hallowed village. Don't think this is going to be an epic chapter. It is easier to get a camel through the eye of a needle than to obtain a passport to Ambridge, let alone a resident's permit. And that's understating things, since all that is necessary to get a camel through a needle is an enlarged needle and a bit of down-sizing with the camel.

It was a case of hello and goodbye to **KARL SWIFT**, the silent phallus. No sooner had he been engaged as keeper by Jeck 'Impeccable Judgement' Woolley, to work in tandem with the most boring and miserable man ever to play the cornet, than we knew we were in trouble. Karl was never around long enough to earn a voice, but he set about the silent Grey Gables staff with heterosexual abandon.

Not content with rogering everyone in sight, he ultimately met his Waterloo when he committed the cardinal sin of greeting Peggoi as 'Peg' – something no one had done since Conn Kortchmar turned up some years ago. Karl's departure was abrupt and involved him running off with someone we'd never heard of who was married to someone else we'd never heard of.

SIOBHAN and TIM HATHAWAY appear to be two characters who are here to stay, so we are just going to have to learn to hate them. Dr Tim comes from Islington, which means he must be a trendy Arsenal supporter, though he is clever enough to realise that in Ambridge you don't mention politics or football (or religion – especially in church). He has had army training and therefore must be able to strangle someone with his bare hands – an attribute that will doubtless enable him to join the ever-growing list of murderers.

Doctors in Ambridge are all too often ridiculously nice to their patients. They have stomach-turningly pleasant bedside manners and a strange habit of making house calls to people with nothing worse than a broken fingernail. They are therefore all undoubtedly impostors, otherwise they would ignore everything their patients said to them, would have repeat visits from people who had come out in rashes due to incorrect prescriptions and would, while themselves reeking of Scotch, tell everyone to stop going to the Bull and rotting their livers.

Unfortunately, they immediately became buddies with Loopy Nigel and Elizabeth, causing a dreadful initial outbreak of cosiness. Wife-swapping possibilities?

PC DAVIES, the 'Community Beat Officer', doesn't say much, but quiet and effective policing is just what a place like

Ambridge needs. It's a case of softly softly catchy murderer, although the scandal is that despite murders on an almost annual basis, the closest we've ever got to a conviction was the travesty of justice that resulted in the acquittal of Fat Man Forrest many years ago. On the rare occasions he does speak, he fits into the identical pattern of all policemen in Ambridge since the friendly Colin Drury, who left some twenty years ago – same belligerent voice, no local accent, insensitive manner, last person you'd call if someone broke into your house.

AMANDA joined the Yoghurt Militia at Bridge Farm. Or did she? What was unusual about her appointment was that, as a general rule when a job is advertised, Jailbird Carter applied for it. But this time someone seemed to arrive spontaneously and, of course, silently. The strange thing is that when Sloane Helen announced she would not after all be going to Zimbabwe, she added, 'which means you won't need a dairy assistant'. Did anyone tell Amanda? Or is she slaving away in the background?

Ironically, it was not until she was meant to be silent that **KIRSTY**, Lancastrian Tommy's girlfriend, discovered she could speak. It would have been a darn sight more convenient if she had kept quiet, because Tommy was not meant to be hobnobbing with her, let alone doing with her what he was doing on the day of the dreaded eclipse. Kirsten has an accent that varies from cockney to broad Yorkshire. She is in essence an eco vandal but she at least claims to be able to recognise skylarks. Listening to them twittering away, she commented to Lancastrian Tommy, 'Makes you realise what we're fighting for.' Well, we simply warn you not to come running to us when the ground is littered with dead triffids and you find yourself covered in skylark dung.

SOLLY AND HEATHER PRITCHARD have to be the most peculiar couple ever to have darkened our nightly doorsteps. Purporting to be the parents of Rooooooth, they are obviously Caribbean and we assume their regrettably protracted visit was *en route* to the Notting Hill Carnival. We know that Solly is not a Geordie because he was heard to utter the words, 'Ye shall have a fishee in a little dishee' which would have been such a racist stereotype of our Tyneside brothers as to render him liable to a ducking in the Am.

SIMON GERRARD is recycled rather than new. As oily as a tin of sardines, he arrived to take up an academic post in the middle of the summer term, which no one seemed to find at all unusual. He is exceptionally odious, smarmy and unpleasant, but we suspect that by the time you are reading this Debbie will have said, 'Yes please, I mean no don't, stay, I mean go away, marry me, no don't' and he will have been up before the courts for 'over enthusiasm' – just as happened to the great Simon Pemberton before him.

A warm welcome to **STEVE HARRIS**, recently moved into Glebelands and is already a key member of the cricket team. Could he be about to become the first speaker to emerge from that silent housing estate?

One of the mysteries of Ambridge is how Grey Gables functions with so few staff. The Village Bicycle suddenly cast some light on the matter in 1999, when she reeled off a list of names – **JULIUS, LUIGI**, **KAREN**, **ALISON** and **JEREMY**. Though we never hear them, it is comforting to know that Trudy Porter, Jean-Paul and Lynda don't have to run the whole place themselves.

BRENDA TUGGER may not be new in town, but she is certainly new in voice. It was the shock of passing an A-level that caused her to speak for the first time in many years. Her previous utterances date back to the halcyon days when she, Sloane Helen and Kate turned Peggoi's Blossom Hill Cottage into a drugs den-cum-knocking shop. Amazingly, her new voice does have a hint of rural accent and is not too ridiculously different from what we might have been entitled to expect from some one who lives in a Midlands village.

FAT PAUL is a welcome arrival into our conciousness and comes from the seemingly endless list of Eddie's friends who he never sees but speaks about in fond tones. Fat Paul managed to put him in touch with a financial advisor who fixed a very generous secured loan – secured against the continuing unbroken nature of Eddie's teeth.

There certainly seems to be room for some more newcomers. At the time of writing, and we realise that these things can be put to rights very quickly, Ambridge seems to have a number of empty properties. No one has moved in to Martha's, or to Fat Man Forrest's, or to Mrs Barraclough's – sound like ideal homes for Clive, Spanner and Craven.

Oh No!
It's Twins!

Each year reaches a nadir of cosiness which to Anarchists is about as welcome as a shining torch to a bat. In 1998 the wedding of Blandvoice and the awful Shul-ugh ran off with the prize. But 1999 offered a rival event, the pregnancy of Elizabeth. No one has been sterile in Ambridge since Pru Forrest and Christine Boring-Johnson, but a Chinese-style sterilisation programme for members of the Archer family would be an act of mercy for thousands of listeners.

The outrage is that most of the parents in Ambridge are completely unfit for the task. They set an appalling example for the rest of the nation. We have Roooooth, who feeds her children on frozen pizzas, crisps and chicken nuggets from the Cash and Carry. Then Shul-ugh, who allows her demonic son to booby-trap his own grandmother. Now Elizabeth, a high-class hooker, is duping poor Nigel into believing himself to be the father of her TWINS.

As with so many Archer pregnancies, there is a scandal surrounding the identity of the father. It is quite amazing that no one has yet tumbled to the fact that Roooooth's Josh was sired by BSE Andy. But there is no question in our minds that the father of Elizabeth's twins can be none other than Horny Hugh. Elizabeth was obviously besotted with Horny Hugh, who paid her vast sums of money for her services. It was evident that she had not genuinely finished her relationship with him, and why should she?

No one can seriously believe that Nigel, whose head must have been shoved down the lavatory at his public school on a round-the-clock basis, could really father children. He could not begin to understand such a complex matter as procreation. Indeed the affection he lavished on the dreaded Ellie May was an indication that he had found his intellectual equal.

With Nigel becoming ever more syphilitic by the day and demonstrating all the tell-tale signs of a thoroughbred, there was never any logic or incentive for her to return to him.

The Anarchist ideal for a reformed Ambridge would see a complete Borsetshire-wide ban on knitting needles and baking materials. This would do a great deal to reduce the unacceptable cosiness quotient. Every time a baby is in the offing, the Foghorn goes completely wool-lally and begins knitting in a manic way.

Births in Ambridge are always attended by a laborious and repetitive sequence of events. Not only do we have to contend with knitting but also the christening. Any Archer baby usually has to wear some moth-eaten old Muzzi that belonged to Doris's aunt's grandmother's goldfish. How they will propose to spread this across twins, we dread to think. Then there's the matter of godparents. With six to find there is even more scope for people to go into great marathon sulks if they are not included. The awful Shul-ugh will expect to be godmother to both. Then there's the question of whether they invite Siobhan to be a godmother or will it be tactless? We would suggest they perm godparents from Baggie, Snatch, Dr Death, Sharon, Alice, Sammy the Cat and the AI man.

The Great Anarchist Challenge

In the grid opposite you will find at least twenty-five *Archers*-related names, words or phrases. Unlike the normal Clarrie-style word-search, with a 3 x 3 grid and the instruction to look for the word 'dog', this is tough – we are giving you just one clue. Each answer is horizontal, vertical or diagonal and you may need to read it backwards. You may find some three-letter words, but the only one we want you to find is TFW (there's the clue). You can ignore any others.

Photocopy your filled-in word-search and send it to the Archers Anarchists (see 'Archers Anarchists: The Next Step' page 171). We will offer one year's free membership of Archers Anarchists to the first twenty-five correct answers we receive, plus consolation prizes of patronising letters to runners-up. The decision (and derision) of the judges is final even if it is wrong and unfair, as it probably will be. Some correspondence may be entered into.

```
G J O P R G J H J K F H H F J K B N J U I O O F V V
J H O R T S Y U I P N G F J I E D D C L A R B G H D
N F R B S E A N D Y H J K Y S H I O C H D F T A A G
Z P O N L P S D F T Y T T Y N G S G W R Y I O P N I
P L B S S A O T D A M F Q L T Z E C C L E S E R E P
D R E C F D N B R O O L A M B R G M R H M G R K T Y
J P S V R I V D L I D R I B L I A J D P G G I G M F
U O N F F W T R V H O M B U C A S T Y O O I I P T W
J R E B K A G K I O T R Z Q U O U L I K Y H A F D Y
O T V I L L A G E B I C Y C L E A P L L O Y O B N G
M I B T P I C X R H S C O O R P S C V I A G A F B E
R A G H T F W C C R A V E N U Y K T Y H H G V B N O
S U S D F H I H K O J C M N G Y E E T O Y Y U T I R
A F R H O I W J S O S S C R T U E V R O O P E L R F
P I H P M H Y F M O B I R P S G L N C R N T T K A L
S T G K I F E S D T H R D H N E D S D F G H K P A G
T A B R O O R K F H I O O L G R N E M T H E L O N L
S C R E T O M T L N E D B E H G A B D N A H T Y M S
P K G R E P L A N M Y G H J R Y K M A D Y T O H O M
K N H A B P G M U F S F U N T Y R R G J L T Y K L P
L I J K B L T E T R A U Q R E K O R C Y M M O T N L
B P P L G Y S A D H T D C U G I P G B H I P S D F I
O E A H G Y H H S G A R T S S H M D H S S C R Q T N
B H T N B Q K U E R P Q I R F G N A D F T F G S O C
H T T M I P T U N D C A R R O P S D D M I S R L S G
G R R A D S N I G T I N F C U C K R F O R P E M B E
```

Archers Anarchists
The Next Step

If you can pass the Aptitude Test on page 18 of this book, you may be a suitable subscriber to the glorious movement that is Archers Anarchists. If you dare, you can apply for further information by sending a stamped addressed A5-size envelope to:

**Archers Anarchists,
15 Hewgate Court,
Henley-on-Thames,
Oxon RG9 1BS.**